1994-1995 ANNUAL

CALIFORNIA GOVERNMENT AND POLITICS

CALIFORNIA JOURNAL PRESS

INTRODUCTION

The California Phenomenon

The California system of government is the same in bold outline as the government of the United States, with three theoretically equal branches of government operating under the supreme law of the land, the Constitution. Nevertheless, there are some significant differences:

• The California Constitution is far more detailed than the United States Constitution and, thus, the Governor and the Legislature have far less power and freedom than the President and Congress. Matters that are left to the statute-writers in Washington are covered in detail in the California Constitution, taking these issues out of the hands of the Governor and Legislature. The judiciary, on the other hand, may be even more powerful because this branch is in charge of interpreting the constitution.

• Normally, the speaker of the Assembly has far more power in Sacramento than any single member of Congress in Washington because this official controls virtually all committee appointments. Few bills pass over the speaker's objection. However the power of particular speakers ebbs and flows depending on factors such as their personalities, the size of their party's majority and the loyalty of their parties caucus.

• The people at large have much more control over California government than over national government because they have the powers of initiative, referendum and recall, giving them the ultimate voice in all matters that are not in conflict with the United States Constitution. Most major fiscal decisions, such as the enactment of general-obligation bond issues and the raising of local taxes, also cannot be made without voter approval.

Other factors make California unique as well. It has been the land of superb climate, breathtaking natural scenery, rapid growth, and the glamor of movie stars and the radio and television industries. Its government and politics reflect the excitement of a land of opportunity and colorful characters, and the news media look to California for the bizarre and offbeat. These unique characteristics may be fading, however. No longer is California the promised land; smog has dulled the horizon; unemployment runs higher than elsewhere; and the movie industry is far from what it used to be. California is experiencing the ills of a mature society: slowed financial growth, reduced national defense spending with the end of the Cold War, declining infrastructure, burgeoning population, especially among new immigrants from foreign lands, and the need for urban renewal. The Los Angeles race riot of 1992 (the worst ever in the nation), sparked by the beating of African-American Rodney King by four white police officers and their acquittal by a Simi Valley jury, is indicative of California's urban malaise. California, in short, is no longer the land of milk and honey.

Constitution

Every few years the California Legislature prints a paperback book with up-to-date versions of the United States and California Constitutions. The document that is the basic law of the entire nation takes up 27 pages; but the California Constitution takes up three times as much space (and twice as much just for the index).

The state constitution contains 21 articles describing, in great detail the bill of rights, the powers of various branches of government and basic state law in such fields as education, local government, corporations, taxation, water, harbor frontages, state debt, homesteading, motor vehicles, civil service, open space, public housing, and even the minimum drinking age.

The California Constitution wasn't always such a long-winded document. The first constitution, adopted in 1849 (one year before California was admitted into the Union), was a basic statement of the rights of the people and the responsibility of the three branches of government. Peter H.

Burnett was elected California's first governor in November 1849, and the first Legislature convened shortly thereafter to levy taxes, establish cities and counties, put the courts into operation, and borrow enough money to grease the wheels of state government. Over the next 30 years, only three major changes were made to this constitution. This stands in sharp contrast to the current practice of adopting amendments every election year.

Massive unrest produced a greatly expanded new constitution in 1879. There was tremendous distrust of the state government, especially the Legislature, and demands were made for greater public control over taxation. The state's population had increased 17-fold in its first three decades. A drought and unfavorable economic conditions had produced mass unemployment. The railroad bloc practically ran the state and was an obvious target. Farmers were in revolt against the railroads and other businessmen. Unemployed whites joined the Workingman's Party to seek a ban against imported Chinese labor. Constitutional reform was seen as a solution, and a convention was called in 1878. The result was an extremely detailed document, which was adopted the next year by a comfortable but not overwhelming margin. The document remains the basic law of California, although it has been amended hundreds of times.

But despite the goals of those who demanded the convention, the second constitution did not provide major reform. That was to come later with Hiram Johnson and the Progressives, who instituted the initiative, referendum and recall.

Amending the Constitution

There are three ways amendments to the California Constitution may be placed on the ballot for approval by a majority of the voters: by initiative petition now requiring over 600,000 signatures of registered voters, by legislative proposal, and by constitutional convention.

• *The initiative.* Almost every election California voters decide the fate of one or more measures placed on the ballot through the initiative process. The initiative was designed as a method of exerting public control over the Legislature, so that bills ignored by the lawmakers could be put into effect. In recent years, elected officials themselves have sponsored initiatives when they are unable to get their way in the Legislature. Beginning in the late 1970's the initiative has been used more and more frequently by special interest groups, the very element the initiative was created to counter. The initiative can also be used to enact statutes.

• *Legislative proposal.* Every year, legislators introduce dozens of proposed constitutional amendments. A small percentage receive the necessary two-thirds vote of each house to qualify for the ballot. A 1983 law requires that ballot measures be numbered consecutively from election to election, starting with November 1982, to avoid confusion. Thus, for example, the November 1990 ballot measures were numbered 124 to 151.

• *Convention.* The constitution provides that the Legislature may call a constitutional convention by a two-thirds vote of both houses. However, it has not done so since 1878. Instead the Legislature has chosen to form a revision commission because it can control the commission and its recommendations. Such a commission existed from 1963 to 1970. The commission had some successes during those years and managed to reduce the size of the constitution considerably. From time to time sentiment is expressed for re-establishing the commission to continue the work of streamlining the state's supreme legal document. 🏛

DAN WALTERS
THE NEW CALIFORNIA
FACING THE 21ST CENTURY
2nd Edition

WITH AN INTRODUCTION BY LARRY BERG

Reprinted from *California Journal*, January 1992

California had scarcely two million citizens in 1909 when Lord James Bryce, British ambassador to the United States, visited the state and asked a prophetic question: "What will happen when California is filled by 50 millions of people and its valuation is five times what it is now? There will be more people — as many as the country can support — and the real question will be not about making more wealth or having more people, but whether the people will then be happier

Dan Walters is a political columnist for The Sacramento Bee *and author of "The New California." This article is a shortened version of Chapter 1 of the second edition of "The New California," due for publication in February.*

or better than they have been hitherto or are at this moment."

Eighty-plus years later, California is more than halfway toward that 50-million mark and has become America's most diverse, most populous and most economically, culturally and politically potent state. But without knowing it, Californians are still seeking answers to Lord Bryce's question as they careen toward the 21st Century.

From San Ysidro to Susanville, from Ventura to Volcano, from Moreno Valley to Moraga, no region of the state is being left untouched as California fashions a 21st Century civilization like nothing ever seen on the North American continent: ethnically complex, with distinct socio-economic classes; competitive; technologically sophisticated; older and more harried; and, unless a cadre of new civic and political leader-

ship emerges, a society that loses its communal identity and evolves into a collection of mutually hostile tribes.

California's once-powerful industrial economy, created during the emergency of World War II and later expanded to serve both Cold War and civilian demands, has given way to a post-industrial hybrid economy that rests on multiple bases and resembles that of a major nation more than that of a typical American state.

In a single generation, hundreds of lumber mills, auto and tire factories, steel plants, canneries, railroad yards, shipyards and other basic industries have closed. Of those that survive, many have downgraded their wage structures to meet foreign competition. Deregulation of trucking, telephone service and airlines has made them more competitive but also has forced

Ethnicity

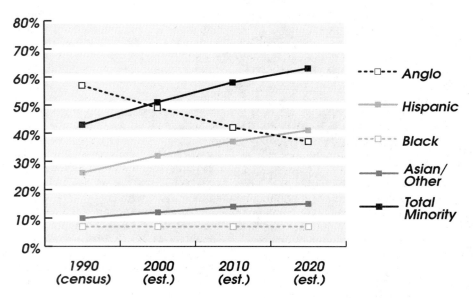

Legend:
- - -□- - - **Anglo**
——■—— **Hispanic**
- - -□- - - **Black**
——■—— **Asian/Other**
——■—— **Total Minority**

X-axis: 1990 (census), 2000 (est.), 2010 (est.), 2020 (est.)

Y-axis: 0% to 80%

their employees to accept lower wages. And the new industrial jobs that have been created, especially those in high-tech and services, are overwhelmingly non-union, with non-professional wage scales in the sub-$12 per hour range.

At the same time, whole new industries have emerged, based on trade with burgeoning Pacific Rim nations, on highly sophisticated technology and on information; new industries that created three million jobs during the 1980s and allowed California to absorb a record increase in population while lowering its unemployment rate before a severe recession took told in 1990.

Between traditional industry's contraction and new industry's expansion lie the seeds of socio-economic stratification. Opportunities for the children of the postwar industrial middle class have been reduced, or at least become more contrasting. They and the young immigrants who continue to pour into California must either prepare themselves for expanding opportunities in technical, managerial, creative and professional fields or be content with relatively low-paying service industry jobs.

California's work force, therefore, is being squeezed like a tube of toothpaste: an expanding overclass at the top, earning the $40,000-plus salaries, buying the homes, living the California

good life; and an exploding underclass at the bottom, ill-educated, ill-served by overburdened social services, struggling to find affordable housing, forgoing medical care and seeing the doors of opportunity become more difficult to open; and an economic and social middle that stagnates or even declines. And it is a change that is punctuated by the state's rapidly evolving ethnic structure, one in which today's minorities will soon become the collective majority. The economic and social differences are likely to become more distinct as California continues to move away from the egalitarian ideal.

Economists Leon Bouvier and Philip Martin, in a mid-1980s peek into California's future for the Washington-based Population Reference Bureau, described that scenario as "the possible emerging of a two-tier economy with Asians and non-Hispanic whites competing for high-status positions while Hispanics and Blacks struggle to get the low-paying service jobs." They noted that since 1970, "employment growth has shifted from high-wage manufacturing and government sectors to the lower-wage trade and service firms that are most likely to hire unskilled immigrants..."

End-of-decade economic data verified their prediction. Between 1982 and 1990, California's manufacturers added about a quarter-million jobs, but the service

and trade sectors created nearly two million. Between 1972 and 1989, manufacturing dropped from nearly 21 percent of the state's jobs to about 17 percent. Jobs at the lower end of the scale ($5000 to $15,000 per year) and those at the upper end ($40,000 to $50,000 per year) grew two to three times faster than middle-income jobs ($25,000 to $30,000 per year). Increasingly, California families have achieved or clung to middle-class status only by merging paychecks of two or more workers.

There are strong indications that these trends will continue in the 1990s. The state Employment Development Department estimates that total California employment will increase by nearly one-third between 1987 and 2000, from 11.7 million to 15.4 million jobs, with above-average increases in trade, finance and services, and sub-par growth in manufacturing, transportation, communication, mining and government categories. The Center for the Continuing Study of the California Economy is even more optimistic, seeing employment in the state approach 17.5 million by 2000 with job and personal-income growth rates in the 1990s that are far above those of the nation as a whole and outstripping even population growth.

"This is probably California's last great growth surge," said economist Stephen Levy of the Palo Alto-based economic study center. "It is entirely possible that the state's population, which will go from 30 million to 40 million in 20 years, may never each the 50-million mark." Levy said that lower birth rates should slow California's population growth after 2010.

There is, however, dissent from some economists who believe that California peaked out in the 1980s and now faces a bleak economic future because of its deteriorating infrastructure and a competitive posture vis-a-vis other states and nations. They have noted a seemingly accelerated abandonment of California by major employers, especially manufacturers, who shift or expand plants in other states and nations because of California's above-average operational costs.

George Salem, a banking analyst for Prudential Securities, created a stir in California economic circles in 1991 when he circulated a report suggesting that the state "shows new evidence of structural weakness" and could face the kind of severe economic dislocation that struck Massachusetts and Texas during the 1980s.

At the time that Salem delivered his startling verdict, the state was experiencing a severe recession, with unemployment having jumped more than 2 percent since the go-go days of the 1980s. During the first year of the recession, from mid-1990 to mid-1991, the state lost an astonishing 380,000 jobs — roughly a year's employment growth during the expansive years of the 1980s. And despite the recession, which economists said was exacerbated by such localized factors as a record freeze and cutbacks in military procurement spending, California continued to experience huge levels of migration and child birth that drove its population upward by some 800,000 persons a year, thus raising doubts whether the state could continue to absorb newcomers or would face a future of continued economic uncertainty.

At the very least, the recession accelerated the evolution from an industrial to a post-industrial economy and thus the stratification of California society.

And if stratification happens, it may set the stage for a 21st Century political climate that pits haves against have-nots, with the political middle declining along with the economic middle and both major parties being compelled to realign themselves to the new socio-economic reality. Lewis Butler and Bruce Kelley of California Tomorrow, an organization devoted to worrying about California's future, use a harsh term to describe what is happening: segregation. This can be avoided, they wrote in 1989, only if people of different classes, colors and cultures live, work and go to school together.

The data of change, gleaned from a variety of public and private sources, is staggering:

• California's population, less than 16 million in 1960, grew by nearly 50 percent to 23.8 million by 1980, hit 30 million by 1990 and is expected to top 36 million by 2000 and climb to more than 40 million by 2010.

• The Anglo population (what demographers call "non-Hispanic white") is virtually stagnant. In fact, the Anglo population may begin to decline before the turn of the century, and a low Anglo birthrate means that its portion of the population is growing older faster than others, with median age already at least 15 years higher than the non-Anglo population.

• Some three-quarters of the near-term population growth and nearly all long-term growth is among Hispanics and Asians. California already is home to more than a third of the Asians who live in the United States, and the proportion of Californians who have Asian ancestry swelled from 4 percent to 10 percent in just a decade, replacing blacks as the state's third-largest major ethnic group.

• The Hispanic population, meanwhile, is being expanded by a high level of legal and illegal immigration from Latin America, mostly Mexico, and by a birthrate that is nearly twice that of Anglos. Demographers expect the continued political unrest and economic chaos in Latin America to push millions of Latino immigrants across a porous border into California, and even economic reform in Mexico will not have a major impact on that trend for years.

• The Black population is relatively stagnant, fixed at under 8 percent of the total; it's not shrinking but grows only at the rate of the overall population.

• Sometime before 2000, perhaps as early as 1996, Anglos will be a minority for the first time — a decade earlier than demographers had expected in the mid-1980s. A generation later, Hispanics and Anglos will be about equal in population, approximately 38 percent each.

• Despite an evening-out of population among the state's large ethnic groups, there are growing disparties in education and economic attainment. Hispanics and Blacks are far more likely to drop out of high school and less likely to obtain college educations than either Anglos or Asians, thereby becoming less able to compete for the well-paying professional and technical jobs that California is continuing to produce.

• With high birthrates among recent immigrants, the overall status of California's children has deteriorated markedly in recent years. A quarter of California's mothers are unwed and disproportionately high numbers of newborn babies suffer from low birth weights, drug addictions and other maladies. And as vaccination rates for children decline, once-conquered childhood diseases such as measles are staging alarming comebacks.

• Some 20 percent of California's 30 million residents lack any kind of health insurance, either private or public. This accounts for 20 percent of the nation's uninsured, even though the state contains just over 12 percent of the American population.

But the signs of change are to be found in more than numbers. They are to be found in the changing California landscape. They are found in such places as Moreno Valley, a small community in the semi-desert of Riverside County, which was the state's fastest-growing county in the 1980s. Moreno Valley just became a city in the mid-1980s and within a few months had a population of more than 100,000, mostly young families. It was graphic evidence of one of the most important social trends of the 1980s: dispersal of the economy and population from coastal enclaves to interior valleys and hills.

That phenomenon was fueled, in part, by the changes in the economy, especially the advent of portable jobs in burgeoning technical and service fields — jobs that do not depend on proximity to raw materials or even to transportation centers and that can be moved out of traditional urban employment centers and into the suburbs, thus allowing workers to move even further into the countryside for more pleasant surroundings and less-expensive housing. The move to the interior is evident from Escondido in northern San Diego through San Bernardino and Riverside counties to the Central Valley as far north as Redding.

It is largely, however, a movement of Anglos. And it contributes, as do continued high rates of immigration, to radical social surgery on the face of California's cities. As whites flee the cities, their places are taken by foreign immigrants who pack themselves ever more densely into stocks of housing that are not expanding.

Los Angeles, the new American melting pot, lost 500,000 Anglos between 1970 and 1980 and is headed for a 60 percent Hispanic population by the turn of the century. There are more than 100 separate languages spoken at Los Angeles area schools, 75 of them at Hollywood High School alone. Conversely, San Francisco, once a polyglot, is becoming a Beverly Hills-like enclave of the Anglo-Asian affluent, driving its middle classes to the suburbs and its Blacks across the bay to Oakland by development policies that favor high-income professionals. One-time farm towns of the Central Valley are diversifying their economies and flirting with metropolitan status.

In addition, whole regions of the

state, especially those north of the San Francisco-Sacramento axis, have seen their basic industries of timber and agriculture decline and nothing emerge to replace them. The result: economic and social stagnation that forces the young to seek jobs in growth areas.

The growth in and changing composition of California's population during the next 30 to 40 years will put an incredible strain on transportation systems, water supplies, sewage treatment, housing supply, educational facilities — what those in the public policy trade call "infrastructure." The California Economic Development Corporation has warned that without a massive overhaul of transportation policies, traffic congestion will increase by 15 percent a year.

Local officials throughout the state, especially in high-growth areas, already feel the strain and are compelled to take extraordinary steps to deal with it. But as they and state officials seek the billions of dollars needed to build and staff public facilities, they collide with another phenomenon that evolved in 1980s California: resistance to new taxes among voters who are not representative of the diverse new California but carry-overs from an earlier era. At the precise moment that California's political leaders confront a society that grows more complex as it grows numerically, California's voters are numerically stagnant, overwhelmingly white, middle-aged and middle-class, with conservative atttitudes toward taxes first felt with the passage of Proposition 13 in 1978 but still being expressed in the 1990s. The effect of these twin, contradictory pressures is to contribute to the political confusion and deadlock that marked the 1980s.

Politicians fear voter backlash if they propose new government programs, or expand old programs due to the pressures from expanded caseloads. And both the state and local governments have direct restraints on spending imposed by a Proposition 13 aftermath (Proposition 4), approved by voters in 1979 and modified only slightly in 1990.

The Legislature, moreover, has become preoccupied with internal power struggles and a series of image-bending scandals. Both it and the governor of the 1980s, Republican George Deukmejian, seemed disinterested in dealing with the far-reaching public policy issues that dynamic socio-economic change creates. Instead, they played games of political one-upsmanship that led to an explosion of initiative ballot measures that also contributed to the state's political paralysis. As the 1990s dawned, many were openly saying that California may have become ungovernable in traditional terms.

That was what Stu Spencer, a veteran Republican political strategist, told U.S. Senator Pete Wilson when Wilson, fresh off a Senate re-election victory in 1988, began thinking about running for governor in 1990. But Wilson, pressured by state and national Republican leaders to run and keep the Capitol in GOP hands for the all-critical reapportionment that was to follow the 1990 census, decided to run anyway. Wilson defeated Democrat Dianne Feinstein, the former mayor of San Francisco, in the November 1990 election. But the fact that both candidates came from the political middle indicated that voters yearned for new leadership.

Wilson came into office in 1991 determined to make California's government work again by shifting emphasis from remedial to preventive in education and social services and by proposing a first-ever statewide growth-management program aimed at bringing some order to the state's chaotic development patterns. But Wilson faced a monstrous state budget crisis born of recession and of a decade of ignoring the conflict between anti-tax fever and huge levels of population growth. He faced, too, a Legislature that was beset by scandal and torn apart by factional and partisan infighting.

As the traditional forms of governance lock up, what may be emerging is a new form of quasi-public, quasi-private governance in which local economic and civic interests, working in concert with local governments, create new vehicles for the improvement of infrastructure. In Santa Clara County, for example, the high-tech industry supported a successful drive to persuade local voters to raise sales taxes to finance better highways after it became apparent that more aid would not be forthcoming from Sacramento. Dozens of other counties followed suit and, in a rare major policy action in the Capitol, Deukmejian and legislators agreed on a comprehensive transportation-financing plan eventually enacted by voters in 1990.

Bond issues, lease-purchase contracts and other forms of creative financing have been used by local officials to finance infrastructure improvements.

But as with other aspects of California culture, it is widening the gap between the haves and the have-nots and weakening the bonds of a broader community. Affluent, growing areas can afford to make such improvements while poor areas with stagnant economies cannot. In 21st Century California, what kind of highways serve motorists, how crowded the schools, how dependable the water supply may depend on where one lives.

The demands of affluent parents for better elementary and high school education got results in Sacramento. But California has continued to lag behind in its overall educational performance, especially in services to the non-affluent, non-Anglo and non-English speakers, as it struggled to cope with record growth in school enrollment. By 1990, the average Latino adult in California had three fewer years of education than Anglo, Asian or Black adults.

Dropout rates among minorities showed little improvement in the 1980s. The community college system, once California's traditional educational ladder for the economically disadvantaged, drifted in the 1980s, a victim of post-Proposition 13 budget restraints and a seeming lack of purpose. Finally, in the late 1980s, there was an effort to revive the system and redirect it back to its original purpose, but no one was certain the reforms would work.

Although California's minority population is growing faster than the Anglo population, the state's public and private universities and colleges remain bastions of Anglo and Asian aspirations. Hispanics, now more than 25 percent of the population, represented less than 10 percent of the undergraduate enrollment at the University of California in 1988, while Blacks were less than 5 percent. Asians were nearly 30 percent of UC's undergraduate enrollment — three times their proportion of the overall population.

California's public schools, anticipating the change that will occur in the larger population a decade years later, acquired a non-Anglo student population in the late 1980s even as they absorbed growth rates that approached 200,000 a year.

But the public school system is producing widely disparate results.

According to the California Postsecondary Education System, only 3.6 percent of 1985's Black high school graduates and 4.9 percent of Hispanic high school graduates were eligible for University of California admission; 13 percent of Anglo graduates and 26 percent of Asians were qualified. Asians, even those who only recently migrated from Southeast Asia, are doing very well in the state's schools — a by-product, sociologists believe, of the Asian cultural impetus to excel that may be missing from other minorities.

The high level of Asian education and economic achievement, markedly above those of the population as a whole, has led many demographers to see them as part of an Anglo-Asian overclass that will dominate California's two-tier society of the 21st Century.

And if the elementary and high schools become dominated by Hispanic and Black students while an aging and stagnant Anglo population produces relatively few school-age children — and sends many of them to private schools — it is questionable whether the overclass will be willing to invest the money in public education. One poll taken for the California Teachers Association indicates that older, white voters are less supportive of public education that other groups; by one estimate, fewer than 20 percent of California voters are parents of public school students and the percentage is declining.

Some Hispanic and Black leaders fear that public education, and especially programs geared to the needs of their children, will be neglected in the 21st Century by a dominant class that has little direct interest in it. Indeed, some see Proposition 13 and its anti-government, anti-tax aftershocks as the first indications of growing disinterest.

Because of myriad pressures, California's political structure in the 1980s seemed incapable of dealing with the change. With professionalization of the Legislature and rising partisanship, the Capitol in the 1980s evolved into a place where the petty concerns of internal politics came to dominate the more pressing needs of the real world. In the largest context, political leaders could not simultaneously meet the needs of the state's large and diverse population and obey the mandates of its politically active and somewhat conservative middle and upper-middle classes.

That tension, which increased steadily during the decade, resulted in an explosion of ballot measures whose fate, both positive and negative, did little to clarify the situation.

If California is evolving into a two-tier society as present trends indicate, it will have vast political consequences. There seems to be an overall swing toward conservatism and the Republican Party in California already. As the state was voting overwhelmingly for President Ronald Reagan's re-election in 1984, for example, it also was giving a plurality of its votes to Republican congressional candidates — despite the fact that a partisan congressional redistricting plan enacted in 1982 handed firm control of the congressional delegation to Democrats.

Pollster Mervin Field reported in 1985 that his survey of voter identification shows the GOP having drawn even with the Democrats for the first time in recent history, a trend that held firm as the 1980s evolved into the 1990s. Democratic voter registration, which approached 60 percent in the mid-1970s, slipped below 50 percent for the first time in more than 50 years.

It seems that Anglo voters and middle- to upper-income Asians and Hispanics are identifying more strongly with the Republican Party. And while they may be outnumbered in the overall population, they are most likely to register and to vote.

Lower-income Hispanics and Asians are not participating in California's political process. Asians have the overall lowest levels of political activity of any ethnic group; by 1990, they were 10 percent of the state's population but scarcely 2 percent to 3 percent of the dependable voters. Blacks are more politically active — and overwhelmingly Democratic — but are a stagnant or even declining portion of the state's population. The industrial middle class, the traditional backbone of the Democratic Party, is shrinking because of economic changes.

These trends create a huge dilemma for the Democratic Party. To appeal to the overclass, it must move its ideological identity to the right, putting less stress on providing government programs to the poor. In doing so, it turns its back on some of its most active constituencies and on the liberal ideological bent of its current leaders. But to organize the unorganized runs the risk of further alienating Anglo, middle-income voters and faces enormous barriers of language, non-citizenship and a lack of political tradition among newly arrived immigrants.

The most likley political scenario for California in the 1990s, and at least the early years of the 21st century, is for dominance by an affluent, politically active overclass using its position to protect its privileges against the larger but weaker underclass. It's a social situation that benefits the Republican Party, which has undergone a quiet evolution into a decidedly more moderate institution as it has expanded its reach. That shift is personified by Governor Wilson, a one-time party pariah for his centrist views. If the Wilsonite philosophy — tough on crime, conservative on taxes and spending; liberal on abortion and environmental issues — becomes the dominant image of the Republican Party, Democrats may be doomed to minority party status in the nation's largest state.

Evolving political power, however, is just one aspect, and probably not the most important one, of a unique culture that continually redefines itself as it expands and diversifies. Clearly, some of California's golden sheen has been tarnished by its social and economic complexities: tangled freeways, high housing prices, rising fear of crime and congested public facilities. A 1989 Field Institute poll revealed a sharp drop in Californians' sense of pride about living in the state. In previous polls, about 75 percent of those responding had rated California "one of the best places to live." But the 1989 poll saw that drop to under 60 percent.

There is some evidence that California's crushing social and economic problems are sinking in on both the state's civic leadership and the larger population. Cadres of civic leaders have been formed, both statewide and at regional and local levels, to explore workable approaches to such pithy issues as regional government, education, water, growth and, most of all, rising levels of social friction.

"California is just entering what may be its most crucial decades since the Mexican War ended in the 1840s," Bouvier and Martin conclude in their study of the state. "The state will never be the same; yet, as with the nation, it remains unfinished. ... The important question is: How will the state adjust to these demographic changes and all their repercussions?"

It's a question whose answer, if anything, is becoming more elusive. 🏛

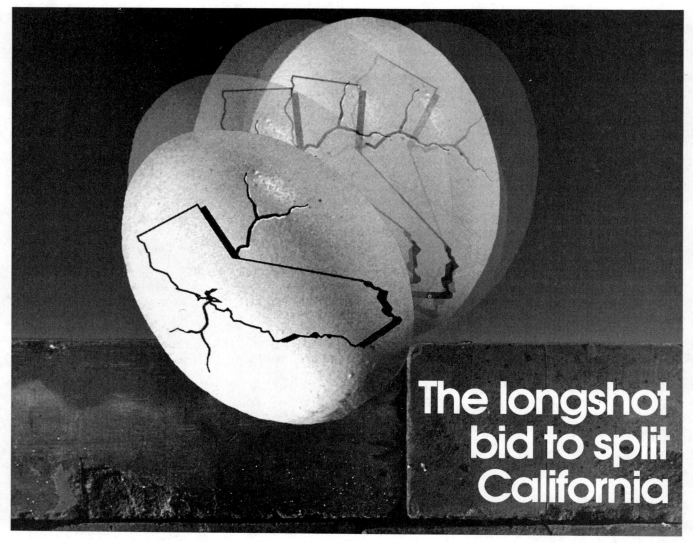

The longshot bid to split California

By CHARLES PRICE

Reprinted from *California Journal* August 1992

*A*cross the globe, political change has come with dizzying speed in the past decade. Gone are the Soviet Union, Yugoslavia and Czechoslovakia, replaced by more than a dozen new nations. Closer to the United States, the province of Quebec is agitating to secede from Canada and form a new, independent nation on our northern border.

Now add to this the movement led

Charles Price is a professor of political science at California State University, Chico, and a frequent contributor to California Journal.

by indefatigable Republican Assemblyman Stan Statham of Oak Run to divide California.

Why divide the state? Statham contends that citizens are intensely frustrated by the gridlock of our present government. "I am proposing a solution. It may not be a perfect solution — but it is worth trying. If you are trying to do a job that is too much for one person, doesn't it make sense to split the job? It is inevitable that we divide."

Statham's is but the latest in a long series of failed split-the-state proposals. While virtually all of the proposals generated in the last 50 years have been launched in the rural north because of southern dominance at the Capitol, earlier this century it was *Southern*

California political leaders who wanted to divide the state because the government was then controlled by *Northern* interests. Other, recent divide-the-state proposals include:

• **(1941) The State of Jefferson.** This was an effort of some local officials from California's northern-most counties to secede and join with southern Oregon counties to form the new state of Jefferson. The outbreak of World War II cut short this attempt.

• **(1965) The States of Northern and Southern California.** This was state Senator Richard Dolwig's plan. His proposal called for dividing the state at the Tehachapi Mountains at the southern end of the San Joaquin Valley. Intriguingly, cities in the south, such as

Santa Barbara and Bakersfield, would have been part of Northern California under this plan.

- **(1970) The states of Eastern and Western California.** This was Democratic (formerly Republican) state Senator Randolph Collier's plan to divide California into two states: the western-urban-coastal; and the rural-interior.
- **(1974) The state of Mendocino.** This was the plan of Robin White and several northern local politicans to divide the state north of San Francisco and Sacramento with the northern portion being called Mendocino.
- **(1978) The state of Alta.** This was the proposal of Democratic state Senator Barry Keene, who, in effect, resuscitated the old Dolwig concept.
- **(1850-?) The state of Nevada.** This has been the long-shared dream of some Lassen County officials. They want their county to divorce California and marry Nevada. Indeed, Peter Lassen, namesake of the county, had formerly served as governor of Nevada. Locals contend with some justification that Reno and Carson City are much closer to Susanville in heart and geography than is Sacramento — particularly in winter months.

Given the previous failures of dividing California, few took seriously Assemblyman Statham's October 1991 call to divide the state. Some viewed the proposal as mainly a warning that rural Northern California was hurting. Indeed, several northeastern counties (Butte and Lassen in particular) face imminent bankruptcy, and most of the others are fiscal basket cases. Rural county officials have bitterly assailed state mandates imposed on them by distant Sacramento pols as the cause of their financial plight.

Others viewed the Statham proposal as a tongue-in-cheek effort to garner some favorable publicity for the veteran assemblyman. After all, for years the plaque on Statham's Assembly office door had read, "Assemblyman Stan Statham, representing the 51st state." Finally, some viewed the Statham plan as a cynical waste of time, diverting attention from California's "real" problems — budget, race, unemployment, water, health care, *ad infinitum.*

Following up on Statham's call for division, the Assembly Office of Research drafted a report to explore the feasibility of the break-up. The report noted, "The state's massive population (nearly 31 million people, followed by New York with 18 million) and geographical size which, in turn, complicate the efficient governing of California as a single unit, is the best argument for splitting the state."

There are two other advantages to division, according to the AOR. One would be to provide California, now grossly under-represented in the U.S. Senate, with two additional members. Another would be to reduce the number of people legislators represent, allowing them to be more attuned to their constituents. (Of course, the present Legislature's size could be doubled or quadrupled, or it could be made unicameral, and it would achieve the same objective of fewer people per election district — without dividing the state.)

Statham's calls for secession initially were met with a strong surge of support in northern counties. The state budget crisis, northern counties' fiscal distress, the Los Angeles riots, environmental restrictions, along with fears of ever-more millions of gallons of water being "expropriated" from Northern California and shipped southward, contributed to their receptiveness. Also, many of the same sentiments that propelled the Ross Perot presidential boom and the anti-incumbent, pro-term limits movements overlap into the divide-the-state, protest effort.

Under the federal Constitution, a state can be divided if the state legislature affected and Congress consent. The single exception to this rule, Texas, an independent nation upon its annexation to the United States, was given the subsequent right to divide into as many as five states if it so chose. Historically, Vermont was carved out of New York, Maine from Massachusetts, Kentucky from Virginia. Of course, all of these splits occurred long ago in the 18th and 19th centuries.

In order to get the state Legislature to approve a split, particularly given the fact that so many legislators represent Southern California constituencies fearful of a cut-off of northern water, Statham decided to apply ballot box pressure. Thus, county boards of supervisors were asked to place a non-binding advisory referendum on their ballots, asking voters whether they favored division. After six months of intense effort, Statham and his staff were able to persuade 31 (out of 58) counties to put the division question on the June 1992 ballot. In eight of these counties a follow-up question was added: If the state were divided, in which portion would you prefer our county to be?

Humboldt was the only far northern county that did not vote on the division question in June. Statham said, "Four of the supervisors in Humboldt County are Democrats, and they saw this as a Republican plot. In San Bernardino County [another non-participant in the referendum], supervisors saw this as a Willie Brown Democratic plot and kept it off the ballot. So, this obviously means that there are some serious DNA deficiencies on these two boards of supervisors." It is important to note that no southern and only some central California counties had the division vote on their June ballots.

To win converts to his cause, Statham hit the media circuit this past spring. He was on nearly 50 radio talk shows (mainly, but not exclusively, in this state), was interviewed on some 25 radio and television shows — including the Home Shopping Network — and his divide-the-state proposal was featured in all of the state's major newspapers and many smaller papers. The concept also has been of interest in foreign newspapers, such as Japan's *Asahi Shimbun* and the *London Times,* as well as Radio Free Europe and the BBC. Dividing the state has been discussed on Rush Limbaugh's nationally syndicated talk show and has provided monologue patter for Jay Leno on "The Tonight Show." Statham also has hired the Stoorza, Ziegaus and Metzger public-relations firm to assist in the effort.

In all, 27 of 31 counties voted in support of a state division.

While most Northern Californians strongly supported division, the 20 northern counties that gave at least 60 percent to the proposal constitute only about 4 percent of state voters. Support dwindled in southern counties.

After reviewing the 31 county voting results in June, Statham decided he had to modify his north-south split into a three-way division of Northern, Central and Southern California. Statham was convinced that Bay Area, Wine Country and San Joaquin Valley counties that had either narrowly approved or voted against separation did so mainly because they did not want to be lumped together with Southern California.

After the vote of the counties, Assembly Speaker Willie Brown an-

North California

Population	2,350,725
Budget	$3.6 billion

Number of counties:	28
Number of states in the U.S. with smaller population:	17
Number of states with smaller budget:	24

Central California

Population	10,146,200
Budget	$15 billion

Number of counties:	22
Number of states in the U.S. with smaller population:	42
Number of states with smaller budget:	47

South California

Population	17,853,900
Budget	$27 billion

Number of counties:	8
Number of states in the U.S. with smaller population:	48/49
Number of states with smaller budget:	48/49

ALTERED STATES

nounced the formation of a select committee to Divide the State to be chaired by Statham to include Republican colleague David Knowles and Democrats Lloyd Connelly, Jack O'Connell and Dick Floyd. The select panel will draft a joint resolution to divide California into three states generally along the guidelines Statham proposed. Each of the three states would

be roughly equivalent in per-capita fiscal resources.

If approved by the Legislature, the division resolution would be placed on the next statewide ballot. If a majority of

voters approve, Congress (both houses) would then be asked to give approval to the three-state division. Once this happens, constitutional commissions would be established in the three Californias to draft constitutions, determine the size of their state legislatures and whether term limits should be imposed, decide on the name of their state and select a capital site. The very earliest this could occur would be in 1995.

Statham believes that his chances of getting a favorable legislative vote will be enhanced by the fact there will be many freshman legislators elected this November. Moreover, state cutbacks in local government funding because of the budget crisis should further fuel secessionist sentiment. Additionally, Speaker Brown has for years supported dividing the state. Brown stated in a recent *Sacramento Bee* article, "It's [division] the only shot I got at governor. I know I don't have a fair shot in Orange County."

Notwithstanding these factors, it will be *very* difficult to get both houses of the Legislature to approve by majority vote the select panel's division maps. Statham's hope is that ambivalent legislators may be persuaded to vote for the resolution because it would have to be submitted to the electorate for majority approval before going to Congress. Certainly, most, but not all, of the handful of northern legislators would be supportive, but whether central and, in particular, southern legislators in sufficient numbers would vote to approve what Statham describes as a "no-fault divorce" is highly questionable.

If the proposal were approved by the Legislature and went on a statewide ballot, most citizens in rural Northern California would be supportive, though some who voted for the split previously as a way of protesting might pull back if they thought it had a chance of succeeding. Statham is convinced that many Central and Southern Californians would be supportive. "If there is any place in the United States that needs to have a new state government so that it can get special attention for all of its internal problems, it is Southern California. They need a legislature all of their own and two U.S. senators who can concentrate 101 percent of their time on gridlocked traffic, dirty air, random shootings and riots."

How Congress might react to a resolution to divide California is not clear.

Mark Powers, Statham's chief of staff, argues that Congress might be likely to dismiss the request if it came solely from the Legislature. But since it would arrive with the backing of the electorate, Congress would have to be more sympathetic.

Non-California House members might find some advantage to splitting the state because it would split the clout of the huge, 52-strong California House delegation. However, given all of the profound ideological/partisan divisions among California House members, they have seldom been a unified force anyway.

The 100 members of the U.S. Senate are members of the nation's most exclusive club. Would they be sympathetic to extending membership privileges to four add-on's? It seems highly unlikely. However, Senate Republicans might be encouraged to be supportive because they would probably gain two U.S. senators from Northern California, but Central and Southern California could counterbalance this by electing Democrats. Finally, if Congress were to agree to a California split, would this not open the door to divide-the-state movements in states like New York, Washington or Kansas? Would Congress want to open this Pandora's box?

Finally, if California were divided into three states, would the lives of Californians be improved? Statham reassuringly argues that water would continue to flow north to south under a three-state format. "Much of the state's water is controlled by the federal government. The only difference would be that water battles would be fought inter-state rather than intra-state." But, would this reassurance allay southern fears? Statham emphasizes that the state's universities, prisons, retirement systems could all be quickly reassigned in a three-state system. "I would prefer for the UC and CSU systems to stay part of one system administered by a three-state compact. But, if the select committee panel decides to break up the system, we could make sure that no out-of-state payments would have to be made for Californians coming from any of the three parts of California." In any case, sorting out the legal nuances could keep lawyers employed for decades.

While there would be some initial start-up costs for new state office buildings and capitols in Northern and Southern California (central would already have Sacramento), Statham is convinced that this would more than be made up for by the chance to begin anew. As an example, "Whether we're talking about David Gardner's salary or the Department of Education and Bill Honig, the problem of our government is it's too top-heavy. Three new California governments would be cheaper than the 142-year-old layers of bureaucracy we now have. We would get to build from the bottom up."

To his credit, Statham has pushed the idea of division farther along then anyone might have expected. At present Statham's "divide-the-state" bill stagnates in the Legislature. Statham is not seeking re-election to the Assembly in 1994. Instead he's running for Lieutenant Governor of the entire state of California.

EXECUTIVE BRANCH & BUDGET

One might think from reading the state Constitution that California's chief executive has absolute authority. In reality, California's governor has, as does the President of the United States, power that is counter-balanced by power of the other branches of government and the electorate. The governor reigns supreme in very few areas. One of them is appointments, but many of these are subject to confirmation by the state Senate. California's governor has remarkably few appointments compared to other states because the civil service system has long been established for all but the top policy posts. The governor also has prime responsibility for the fiscal affairs of state, but his budget is subject to alteration by the Legislature. The governor can reduce or eliminate items in the budget passed by the Legislature. This "line-item" veto is a very powerful tool of California Governors. These vetoes, like any others, are subject to override by two-thirds vote of the Senate and Assembly, through this happens only rarely. Former Republican Presidents Ronald Reagan and George Bush supported a line-item veto federal amendment to strengthen the executive's fiscal power. Democratic President Bill Clinton is also an admirer of the line-item veto.

Governors are elected for four-year terms, with a two-term maximum (established by Proposition 140 in November 1990). Historically, only Earl Warren was elected more than twice. The order of succession is the lieutenant governor, Senate president pro tempore, Assembly speaker, secretary of state, attorney general, treasurer and controller. The governor serves as the ceremonial chief of state, as president of the University of California Board of Regents and the State University and Colleges Board of Trustees, as unofficial leader of his party, and as the head of most administrative agencies through his subordinate appointees. The governor is deeply involved in the legislative process, through presentation of the budget, the office's veto power and the traditional presentation of a package of bills constituting a legislative program (and usually outlined in the annual "state-of-the-state" message). When stymied by the legislature, Governor Pete Wilson has also authored initiatives.

Veto power

The veto is perhaps the governors most potent weapon, but it is essentially a negative power. Governors usually wield considerable influence with members of their own party (because they often control the party structure, weak as it is, and because lawmakers like to stay on the good side of a governor so they can get projects for their districts and appointments for their friends). Consequently, vetoes are rarely overridden. When Governor Ronald Reagan had a veto overridden during the 1973-74 session, it was the first over-ride since 1946. Jerry Brown was overridden during his first term on a death-penalty measure and overrides became almost commonplace in 1979, especially on fiscal issues. Neither George Deukmejian nor Pete Wilson has had a veto overridden.

Governors have the power to organize the administrative agencies of state government as they see fit, although the Legislature can veto major reorganization plans. Reagan organized his administration into four agencies headed by the secretaries of health and welfare, business and transportation, agriculture and services, and resources. The Department of Finance reported directly to the Governor. The cabinet met regularly and established policy for the administration.

The Jerry Brown administration employed the case-study method for solving problems and establishing policies. Cabinet sessions at the start were frequent, lengthy and argumentative — far less business-like than in the Reagan years. However Brown put agency executives on a loose leash once they learned what he expected from them. Jerry Brown created a fifth agency, the Youth and Adult Correctional Agency.

George Deukmejian, it was assumed, would be willing to bargain and compromise with the legislature on issues since, as a former legislator, he was used to a give and take process. His unyielding stance during his first year in office on issues like taxes and community college fees surprised many. Despite the fact that he was the sole Republican among the state's statewide officeholders and both houses of the Legislature were Democratic-controlled, Deukmejian wielded the powers of his office with considerable effect.

Deukmejian's Republican successor, Governor Pete Wilson, selected a more moderate and pragmatic group of Cabinet secretaries. Wilson also established a sixth new cabinet and agency: environmental protection, similar to one created administratively by Deukmejian.

Sharing executive power with the governor are a

number of boards and commissions. The governor appoints most of their members and they in turn exercise independent authority. Among them:

University of California of Regents. Aside from the power of the purse, the Regents control the university system.

State University Trustees. This board has less power and prestige than the UC Regents but has been seeking increased independence.

Public Utilities Commission. The PUC sets rates for public utilities and also exercises allied responsibilities.

Franchise Tax Board. This board administers the state income tax and handles other revenue matters.

State Lands Commission. This commission exercises control over the state's oil-rich tidelands and other public properties.

Fair Political Practices Commission. This powerful agency was created by voters in June 1974 to police the state's Political Reform Act covering lobbyist activities, campaign contributions and conflicts of interest.

Energy Resources, Conservation and Development Commission. This commission also went into operation in 1975. It is charged with establishing overall state power policy and with the selection of sites for new power plants.

Agricultural Labor Relations Board. This agency supervises management-labor activities for the agricultural industry.

Lottery Commission. Created by the 1984 initiative to run what is, in effect, one of the nation's largest businesses.

Citizens Compensation Commission. This governmental unit was established by voters with the adoption of Prop. 112 of June 1990. This commission is charged with setting the salary level of all state elected officials except judges.

In a special category is the *State Board of Equalization,* composed of the state controller and four members elected by district. It collects the sales tax and other levies, and supervises county administration of the property tax. From time to time, governors propose elimination of the Board of Equalization and the Franchise Tax Board in favor of creating a Department of Revenue under the governor's control.

Statewide offices

In addition to the governor, the state Constitution requires the election of seven other statewide officials. All are limited to two four-year terms by Proposition 140 (except for the Insurance Commissioner whose office was created after the initiative was drafted). See box for a list of current incumbents, the individuals they defeated and their predecessors.

Here is a brief rundown of the duties of these other statewide officials:

• **Lieutenant Governor:** presides over the Senate, serves as a member of numerous state boards and commissions, and exercises the powers of chief executive when the governor leaves the state or is incapacitated.

• **Secretary of State**: the state's chief election officer; maintains all the state's official files and historical documents, including articles of incorporation; receives lobbyists' registrations and their monthly reports; receives campaign-contribution and conflict-of-interest disclosure forms.

• **Attorney General**: the state's chief law enforcement officer, legal advisor to state agencies.

• **Treasurer**: provides all banking services for the state, including sale of bonds and investment of securities.

• **Controller**: the principal accounting and disbursement officer for the state; administers inheritance and gift taxes and performs a variety of functions assigned by the Legislature, including publication of statistics on local government.

• **Superintendent of Public Instruction**: heads the state Department of Education, but most of the public schools are administered by local boards; state education policy is established by the state Board of Education, composed of gubernatorial appointees.

• **Insurance Commissioner**: This is a relatively new position created by the passage of Proposition 103 in 1988.

Constitutional Officers

	Incumbent (year first elected)	Defeated Nov. 1990	Predecessor
Governor	Pete Wilson (R) 1990	Dianne Feinstein (D)	George Deukmejian (R)
Lieutenant Governor	Leo T. McCarthy (D) 1982	Marian Bergeson (R)	Mike Curb (R)
Secretary of State	March Fong Eu (D) 1974	Joan Milke Flores (R)	Edmund G. Brown Jr. (D)
Attorney General	Dan Lungren (R) 1990	Arlo Smith (D)	John Van de Kamp (D)
Treasurer	Kathleen Brown (D) 1990	Tom Hayes (R)	Tom Hayes (R)
Insurance Commissioner	John Garamendi (D) 1990	Wes Bannister (R)	— none —
Controller	Gray Davis (D) 1986	Matt Fong (R)	Kenneth Cory (D)
Superintendent of Public Instruction	(nonpartisan)	Louis (Bill) Honig*	Wilson Riles

Note: Minor-party candidates omitted.   *Vacated office upon conviction of a felony March 1993

CALIFORNIA EXECUTIVE BRANCH ORGANIZATION

ELECTED CONSTITUTIONAL OFFICERS

Lieutenant Governor
Secretary of State
Controller
Treasurer
Board of Equalization (4)
Attorney General (Department of Justice)
Superintendent of Public Instruction (Department of Education)
Insurance Commissioner

EDUCATION POLICY BOARDS

Board of Education
U.C. Board of Regents
State College and University Trustees
Community College Board of Governors
Postsecondary Education Commission
Commission for Teacher Preparation and Licensing

GOVERNOR

BUSINESS, TRANSPORTATION AND HOUSING AGENCY

Dept. of Alcoholic Beverage Control
Dept. of State Banking
Dept. of Corporations
Highway Patrol
Dept. of Housing and Community Development
Dept. of Motor Vehicles
Dept. of Real Estate
Dept. of Savings and Loan
Dept. of Transportation
California Housing Finance Agency
Stephen P. Teale Data Center
Office of Traffic Safety

RESOURCES AGENCY

Dept. of Conservation
Dept. of Fish and Game
Dept. of Forestry & Fire Protection
Dept. of Boating and Waterways
Dept. of Parks and Recreation
Reclamation Board
S.F. Bay Conservation and Development Commission
Dept. of Water Resources
California Conservation Corps
Colorado River Board
Coastal Commission

HEALTH AND WELFARE AGENCY

Dept. of Alcohol and Drug Programs
Employment Development Dept.
Dept. of Developmental Services
Dept. of Health Services
Dept. of Mental Health
Dept. of Rehabilitation
Dept. of Social Services
Dept. of Aging
Office of Statewide Health Planning & Development
Emergency Medical Services Authority
Health & Welfare Data Center
Dept. of Economic Opportunity

STATE AND CONSUMER SERVICES AGENCY

Fire Marshall
Franchise Tax Board
Dept. of General Services
Personnel Board
Dept. of Consumer Affairs
Public Employees Retirement System
Teachers' Retirement System
Dept. of Veterans Affairs
Dept. of Fair Employment and Housing
Building Standards Commission
Museum of Science and Industry

TRADE AND COMMERCE AGENCY

World Trade Commission
California Film Commission
Office of Tourism
Office of Small Business Development

YOUTH AND ADULT CORRECTIONAL AGENCY

Board of Prison Terms
Dept. of Corrections
Board of Corrections
Prison Industries Authority
Youthful Offender Parole Board
Dept. of Youth Authority

ENVIRONMENTAL PROTECTION AGENCY

Air Resources Board
Integrated Waste Management Board
Water Resources Control Board
Dept. of Toxic Substance Control
Dept. of Pesticide Regulation
Office of Environmental Health Hazard Assessment

SECRETARY OF FOOD AND AGRICULTURE

DEPARTMENT OF FINANCE

DEPARTMENT OF INDUSTRIAL RELATIONS

SECRETARY OF CHILD DEVELOPMENT AND EDUCATION

Office of Administrative Law
Office of Planning and Research
Office of Emergency Services
Office of Personnel Administration
Military Department
Office of Criminal Justice Planning
State Public Defender

INDEPENDENT COMMISSIONS

Agricultural Labor Relations Board
Arts Council
Lottery Commission
State Lands Commission
Coastal Commission
Fair Political Practices Commission
"Little Hoover" Commission
Public Employment Relations Board
Transportation Commission

The commissioner oversees the operations of the state Department of Insurance and has wide authority to approve or disapprove many types of insurance rates.

State Finance

The governor is required by the state Constitution to present a budget each January — an estimate of the state's expenditures and revenues for the fiscal year starting the following July 1st. In a state growing as fast as California, the budget increases dramatically no matter who is governor.

During the eight years Ronald Reagan was governor, the total budget doubled from $5 billion to $10 billion. Jerry Brown's first budget (1975-76) totaled $11.4 billion, and his final budget (1982-83) totaled $25.3 billion. George Deukmejian's first budget (1983-84) totaled $26.8 billion and his last budget (1990-91) was $51.4 billion. Governor Pete Wilson's first budget was $56.3 billion.

These figures can be misleading because they do not show how much the cost of state government has risen. Many of the increases were for the exclusive purpose of relieving-pressure on the property tax or on local government, especially after the passage of Proposition 13 in 1978. In fact, about two-thirds of each year's budget consists of allocations to schools and other elements of local government, and about half the state budget is for public education.

Budget process

The budget process in the Legislature involves detailed study of items that are questioned by the Legislature's fiscal specialist, the legislative analyst. For months, subcommittees of the Senate Budget and Fiscal Review Committee and the Assembly Ways and Means Committee pore over the budget and decide which items should be increased, reduced, added or eliminated. Eventually, the budget is packaged by the fiscal committees and sent to the floor of each house. As a practical matter, either the Senate or the Assembly bill becomes the vehicle for enactment of a budget. The first house to act sends its version of the bill to the other, which then puts its own figures into the legislation and sends it back to the house of origin. The changes are routinely rejected, and the budget is placed in the hands of a conference committee composed of members of both chambers. Even though the constitution requires that the budget be sent to the governor by June 15th, it is often much later before both houses are able to adopt a compromise because passage by a two-thirds majority is required.

Revenue

One major portion of the budget — estimated revenues — is not considered at all by the Legislature, except to verify that funds will be sufficient to meet anticipated expenditures.

The difference between revenues and expenditures (with any carryover from the previous year taken into account) produces the projected surplus for the fiscal year.

About 75 percent of the revenue goes into the state general fund. The remaining 25 percent is collected from specific sources and placed in special funds (notably the motor vehicle fund) to be spent for specific purposes. Estimates in the governor's proposed budget for the 1994-95 fiscal year show anticipated revenue from all funds of $54.8 billion ($41.1 billion general fund; $13.7 billion special funds). Specific fund sources and their percent of total revenue are as follows:

Personal income tax, $18.6 billion (33.9%);
Sales tax, $15.8 billion (28.9%);
Bank & corporation taxes, $5.1 billion (9.3%);
Insurance, $1.2 billion (2.3%);
Motor vehicle (inc. gas tax), $7.2 billion (13.8%);
Tobacco, $650 million (1.2%);
Liquor, $277 million (0.5%);
Estate taxes, $496 million (0.9%);
Horse racing fees, $109 million (0.2%);
Other, $5.2 billion (9.6%).

Expenditures

Total proposed 1994-95 expenditures are $52.5 billion, not counting bond funds. Here are the major items of expenditure as proposed by the governor in January 1994:

Aid to schools K-12, $17.2 billion (32.7%);
Health and welfare, $14.3 billion (27.2%);
Higher education, $4.3 billion (8.3%);
Business, transportation and housing, $4.0 billion (8.0%);
Local government, $3.0 billion (5.8%);
Youth and adult corrections, $3.8 billion (7.2%);
Other, $5.9 billion (11.0%).

While the Legislature can revise the budget in any way it sees fit, the governor has only two choices when he receives the bill act at the end of June: he can veto it in its entirety and thus force the Legislature to pass a new bill, or he can reduce and eliminate specific items (this is known as blue-penciling the budget through line-item veto). This latter is the practice traditionally used.

Until the budget is enacted, the Legislature cannot pass appropriations measures unless the governor provides a letter saying that the expenditure is needed on an emergency basis. Once the budget is passed, however, the Legislature can — and usually does — send the governor numerous bills containing appropriations. The governor can cut the entire appropriation or reduce the amount. (Each of these bills can contain only a single appropriation.)

Pete Wilson:

Steering through a sea of woes

By Richard Zeiger

photos by Rich Pedroncelli

Reprinted from *California Journal*, April 1992

PETE WILSON IS WEARING THE SHEEPISH LOOK he gets when engaged in an activity that may not be dignified enough for the governor of the nation's largest state. He is about to tack a sign to his office door saying, "No Smoking." The effort, accompanied by a raft of television cameras, is to publicize his new executive order banning smoking from all state office buildings. The event is of dubious significance, since most state departments had already eliminat ed smoking and the most prominent exception, the state Capitol itself, is under the control of the Legislature and thus outside of Wilson's domain.

But if the action will have less than cosmic significance, it does succeed in one major respect: It gets Wilson a few precious moments on television news.

Indeed, the Wilson handlers are so enchanted with the motif that they repeat it several days later when Wilson proclaims the official end of the state's six-year drought by posting a new sign over the drought-emergency office, identifying it now as the water-conservation office. Wilson stages the event despite the fact that a day earlier, by mistake, bureaucrats within the state had confessed that the drought had indeed ended, thus stealing their boss' thunder. No matter; the television cameras roll again.

Welcome to the start of Pete Wilson's 1994 re-election campaign.

There has been no formal announcement, of course, but Wilson concedes, "I suppose we have been a little bit more visible."

Although it may seem a trifle premature to be campaigning with the election 20 months away, Pete Wilson has a very long way to go. Indeed, there are many who believe it is all but impossible for Wilson to win a second term, which would make him the first one-term California governor in more than 50 years. Culbert Olson managed it by losing to Earl Warren in 1942.

But Wilson's standings in the public opinion polls remain at an all-time low despite a recent upturn. With the state's economy stubbornly refusing to rebound and with

prospects good for another budget crisis this summer, it could take an extraordinary change of luck for Wilson to survive. And so far, just about all of Wilson's luck has been bad. As governor, he has been faced with a series of natural and man-made disasters of biblical proportions: fires, earthquakes, drought, floods and even urban rioting.

To make matters worse, the national recession and post-cold war cutback in military spending have hit the state with a fury unknown since the Great Depression. In the post-Proposition 13 era, the state's revenue stream has become unusually sensitive to changes in the economy. The property tax is fairly stable even in bad economic times, but the sales and income taxes — the state's major sources of money — fall off rapidly in bad economic times, and Wilson and the state Legislature have been faced with one intractable budget deficit after another.

And chances are good that the same thing might happen again. Democrats and Republicans remain far apart on key issues. Wilson hopes that the new freshman class will be more receptive to making what he describes as the "necessary tough decisions." But some early Wilson deadlines for budget cuts have come and gone, and so far there has been no indication that the new Legislature is any more willing to bend to the Wilson will than was the old one.

Wilson agrees that "in one sense" he has been the victim of bad luck. But the circumstances of his first term, and his reaction to them, have left him "with a story to tell. When it's told and people begin to appreciate it and think about it they will come to the same conclusion: That in fact it's been a time of unrelenting challenges of all kinds and that they have indeed been tough times but they've been met pretty well."

"You have to be aggressive about getting the story out. That is what we haven't done," Wilson said in an interview with *California Journal.*

But if the times were difficult, Wilson's response hasn't always been consistent. In his first year, to deal with the deficit by cutting a deal with legislative Democrats, he accepted substantial increases in taxes and, in exchange, Democrats agreed to some cuts in programs. But portions of the deal also were cobbled together with questionable fiscal gimmicks, and the budget began to unravel before the year was out. Moreover, the conservative faction in Wilson's own party, never really fans of Wilson's to begin with, were angered further by the tax increases. When Wilson's first year ended, the governor seemingly was without a friend in the world.

The second year was not much better. Wilson decided there was little political or practical advantage in combining with Democrats on the budget, and that the worsening financial situation made it impossible and inadvisable to try and balance the budget with more taxes. So Wilson hunkered down. He had learned the lesson that the governor who is willing to say "no" to the Legislature can have the upper hand. Wilson for the most part refused to parley with legislative Democrats, and this led to a budget impasse that lasted more than two months but that was largely settled on Wilson's terms.

"What I understand very well is that while the public is inclined to say, 'A plague on both your houses,' the Legislature is an abstraction to them. They never connect that good old Charlie that they keep re-electing is part of the problem. By contrast, the governor . . . is almost by definition high-profile. If they're not happy with something, he's likely to get a major share of the credit," Wilson offered.

Democrats, he maintained, were willing to hold up the budget in order to gain political advantage. "They haven't even been subtle about it. The speaker [Willie Brown] even indicated in a *New York Times* profile on me . . . it was his purpose to deny me re-election."

But in saying now that he always knew he would get the worst end of a budget impasse, Wilson is indulging in a little revisionist history. At the time, the administration thought that Wilson was in the better position to sit out the

storm. After all, it was the legislators, mostly Democrats, who were up for election in November 1992. The governor wouldn't have to face voters for more than two years. By that time, these budget difficulties would surely be history.

An election debacle

Things didn't quite work that way. The '92 budget fracas was followed by November elections that gave Democrats a resounding victory. They captured both seats in the U.S. Senate, including Wilson's old Senate seat with a victory over John Seymour — Wilson's hand-picked successor; secured the state's electoral votes for Bill Clinton; gained a seat in the state Assembly despite a new reapportionment plan drawn by the state Supreme Court that was expected to benefit Republicans; and managed to defeat Wilson's initiative measure to cut welfare spending while increasing his own powers as chief executive.

All-in-all, it was a dismal showing for Wilson and added to the notion that his re-election prospects are dubious. There was even some talk that he might be subject to a challenge from within his own party. The names of a few conservative challengers were floated, including that of Bay Buchanan, an unsuccessful primary contestant for state treasurer in 1990 and the sister of erstwhile columnist and presidential candidate Pat Buchanan, and that of former Assemblyman Tom McClintock, who

A recent round of base closures added to Wilson's woes

seems to be in favor despite the fact that he was defeated in a 1992 bid for Congress.

Most of that talk died down following last month's Republican state convention as the GOP came to realize that, if it wasn't in love with Wilson, it did like controlling the governor's office.

"When you've lost the White House and you find your governor down 16 points in the Field Poll, it reminds you of why you need to stick together," notes Republican consultant Sal Russo.

But even if Wilson manages to avoid a strong challenge from within his own party, he won't be so lucky in the general election. The Democrats have an array of candidates available to challenge Wilson, and polls at this point show them beating the incumbent.

The favorite of the political cognoscenti at the moment is state Treasurer Kathleen Brown. The daughter of former Governor Pat Brown and the sister of former Governor Jerry Brown, Kathleen already has put more than $2 million in the bank that could be the start of a run for governor. In addition, during the 1992 elections, she campaigned tirelessly for an array of Democrats, assistance that should be repaid in 1994 if she decides to run. Brown possesses the charm of her father and the intelligence of her brother and, at least so far, has not displayed the drawbacks of either.

However, Wilson supporters say that can't last forever.

"Kathleen Brown is an unknown commodity. The more she's known, the less strong she becomes," offers Republican consultant Ray McNally. "Kathleen Brown has nowhere to go but down, and Pete Wilson has nowhere to go but up. It's dangerous to predict Pete Wilson is a one-term governor."

Kathleen Brown has nowhere to go but down, and Pete Wilson has nowhere to go but up. It's dangerous to predict Pete Wilson is a one-term governor.

In addition, the Wilson crew says that Brown isn't well-known to the public. As voters get to know her better, chances are many will not like what they see, particularly if they have some help from a Wilson campaign. They also scorn Brown for what they claim is her failure to take a stand on tough issues.

"Take the sales-tax extension. She says it should be firmly on the table for discussion. There's a tough position," notes Wilson communications director Dan Schnur.

Furthermore, Brown still must make it through a presumably contested primary. Her most likely opponent is state Insurance Commissioner John Garamendi. Also bright and attractive, Garamendi was the titular head of Bill Clinton's California campaign. Even so, Garamendi probably has fewer chits for 1994. For one thing, Garamendi used up some of his capital trying to win his wife, Patty, a seat in Congress. She lost, in her third try for public office, and that defeat may have included the added burden of hobbling her husband's bid for advancement.

But the Almighty rarely makes such blatant interventions in the affairs of mankind, and Wilson likely will face much more formidable opposition.

And Wilson is no pushover. Beneath a placid exterior is a rock-hard campaigner; the Marine who refuses to know when he's licked.

"He's determined and very proud. And he's often underestimated. He welcomes the fact that he'll be judged an easy mark," notes Larry Thomas, a Wilson confidant who worked for the governor when he was still mayor of San Diego. Plus, said Thomas, there are the "inherent powers of the office that can be used to achieve goals and to capture the public attention. He's a man who's skilled at doing that, particularly if he get a little running room from the problems that have been plaguing the state."

Wilson has also been making staff changes, and observers now believe that he has a team in place that is up to the re-election challenge. Indeed, staff difficulties in the beginning of Wilson's administration have been cited as the cause of some of the governor's problems.

"I don't think he's been well-served," notes one Republican observer, who asked to remain anonymous. "He's got some fine people, but by and large, there have been too many screw-ups."

Wilson brought in George Dunn and Joe Shumate and deputy chiefs of staff, as well as Republican hit-man Joe Rodota to be his cabinet secretary. Furthermore, Schnur has hit his stride as Wilson's chief spokesman, a task that had been conspicuously missing after the untimely death in 1991 of Wilson confidant Otto Bos.

Wilson also has refined his position on the economic front. No more finding the middle road that characterized his first year. Now Wilson's mantra is that the state must do all it can to create jobs in the private sector. That means changing the worker's compensation system and giving tax breaks to industry. And it means that a long-awaited Wilson proposal on managing growth in the state turned out to be a tepid rehash of existing policies along with a plea for streamlining the state's various permit processes so that growth can continue. Indeed, there are even some in the environmental community, where Wilson has long been considered one of the few reliable Republicans, who believe the governor is now willing to soften state environmental laws if it will spur business development.

Wilson's own personality should also be given some of the blame. Wilson is good at standing firm, but such a position makes one inflexible. And when events don't go as you plan — as they have not in the first two years of the Wilson administration — a little flexibility might be useful.

Events have forced Wilson to be a governor playing defense. That's not what he had in mind when he got elected. Wilson came to office promising to be one of the most active governors in recent state history. His program of preventive care for children of all economic stripes was novel and aggressive. Indeed, his was the notion that every child should have a "mentor" to help him or her get through the difficult business of growing up. The concept that government would help find everyone a guardian, at its core, can be considered very un-Republican, but Wilson doesn't see it that way.

"The kinds of things that are necessary to give kids the best break in life include those things that are governmental programs like health care for poor mothers, pre-natal care . . . and the entire range of early childhood programs we have instituted," says Wilson. "There has to be an individual, some individual to get them off in life and really to carry them on through."

"I don't think it's a partisan activity," Wilson notes. Lots of volunteer groups already are in the business, and government should be supporting these. "There are hundreds of organizations like this and there should be more."

But the budget crisis has kept Wilson from all but a token start to his new programs; a promise that, one day, things might get better. But for now, Wilson has been the unluckiest of recent governors, and now it just could take a substantial change in fortune for him to survive, although Wilson doesn't see it that way.

"It's easy to govern in easy times."

"I'm not counting on that," Wilson said.

"You make your own luck. People do win re-election who had re-elect negatives that caused people to write them off. Those things change when you have someone to run against.

Budget negotiations with legislative leaders mostly produced gridlock in 1992

"It's easy to govern in easy times. It's difficult to govern in difficult times. You are probably a better governor when you are compelled to manage well and lead in difficult times. It's a hell of a lot more difficult to do.

"The best way to run for any office . . . is to simply do the best job possible with the one you've got. That's what gives you the greatest credibility. Talk is cheap. It is very easy to make promises and it is very difficult for people to judge; they may want to believe the promises but in fact what is most credible to them is what should be — what you've actually done." 🏛

Defense conversion

Can you make a buck when peace breaks out?

Illustration by Rob Wilson

Reprinted from *California Journal*, January 1994

By Mary Beth Barber

The term "defense conversion" is thrown around a lot in Sacramento and Washington, D.C., these days. And the term applies not only to the military itself but to private industries that have been built around defense contracts, including aerospace companies. California lays claim to the lion's share of defense contractors, which proved a gold mine during the Cold War's defense-industry boom but since has turned into pyrite as the federal government cuts back on military spending. Southern California has been especially hard hit, and political leaders have proposed programs to help the state's high-tech industry deal with cancelled contracts and a shrinking aerospace market.

Most industry officials agree that the era of plentiful, high-paying aerospace jobs and large government contracts now is over, and that defense-related industries must tighten their belts, hold onto at least part of the market that might be around in the next decade or so, and seek a new line of business.

Among the most vulnerable defense contractors are the aerospace companies. After all, there isn't much of a private, general marketplace for, say, a supersonic fighter jet. And although aerospace companies now talk about finding a "niche" in the high-tech construction world, each company pursues its own balance between weaponry and commercial ventures. Northrop Corporation, for instance, dips a toe now and then into the commercial field if the opportunity arises, but plans to continue to focus on defense contracts "because we feel it's what we know best," said Northrop's Jim Hart.

Rockwell International, on the other hand, already had a sizable number of non-DOD clients and has looked overseas for customers, including Australia and Korea, said Rockwell's Chris Rodriguez. "We've been focusing on foreign markets for some time," he said, "but we're not necessarily converting from defense. We're expanding." Some of the expansion is still in defense, to other countries besides the United States. But Rockwell has to go outside the defense realm to survive, said Rodriguez.

Lockheed seems to want to stay in the defense industry, continuing with federal contracts like the one to build the F-22 fighter. General Dynamics bowed out completely, selling that portion of its company that dealt with defense contracts to Hughes and leaving behind close to 3000 workers in San Diego. Other companies have looked to satellites, NASA or private airlines to gain business — although even that has proved to be dangerous. For example, more than 200 recently displaced workers from Aerojet in Sacramento may lose their jobs in Iuka, Mississippi, because NASA cancelled the company's contract for the Advanced Solid Rocket Motor Program, designed to replace the solid boosters responsible for the destruction of the shuttle spacecraft, Challenger.

The term "defense conversion" may be a misnomer, said one industry representative, and may not be possible in pratical terms. Delco-Remy project manager Jeffery Owens told PBS' investigative news program, "Frontline," that "it's an unnatural act to instill commercial mentality on a military business." As Rodriguez noted about Rockwell, companies aren't trying to wholly convert from defense contracts into other areas but instead are cautiously investigating other industries that closely resemble their own. Aerospace companies are just doing what they need to survive, as any business would, and unnecessary risk is not a survival technique. It's better to have a smaller company than no company because of an unnecessary risk. But smaller companies mean less employees, especially high-wage technicians and engineers. Just about every defense contractor has downsized over the past five years, most letting go a significant number of people with relatively high salaries.

Aerospace workers averaged over $18 per hour, and many of those unemployed now are middle-aged with families to support and bills to pay. The little investment that aerospace companies are doing outside of defense contracts won't solve the unemployment problems, said industry officials. While the executives believe their particular company will survive, they aren't expecting to be able to hire anywhere near the number of workers they had before. Displaced engineers and technicians go to the unemployment lines, competing for a limited — and dwindling — number of aerospace jobs.

Some aerospace companies want to build their strength in related fields. "We'll look into new business areas — cautiously — and only when we find a fit with our core technologies, and with a well established company," said Hart. For example, Northrop is heading up a team of 18 companies to design a bus for Los Angeles' Metropolitan Transit Authority. And although the contract is for $3.8 million, it amounts to small change compared to Northrop's annual $5.5 billion in sales. And Northrop is a medium-sized aerospace company, noted Hart, not one of the giants. "Those jobs we've been losing in defense over the past couple of years aren't going to be replaced by contracts like that," he warned.

The effects on the state's economy can be devestating, and the handful of high-technology projects the government offers defense contractors isn't enough to make up for the losses, said Adrian Sanchez, regional economist for First Interstate Bank Corporation. "Think of the billions of dollars [the federal government] was investing before," he said. "The type of money that they're talking about isn't going to put a dent in California's problems." All industries go through restructuring, but California had the bulk of the defense industry — an industry that relied on federal dollars rather than the open market. Fewer aerospace workers taking home hefty paychecks means fewer dollars being spent in the state. "I think the economy will come back," said Sanchez, but it will take some time.

Aerojet's Martha Alcott pointed out that defense downsizing has happened in the past, especially after the Korean and Vietnam wars. The difference this time is the general economy, especially of California. "I think Sacramento has a lot of engineers who were laid off in the '60s ... who became entrepreneurs," she said.

But Alcott also pointed out that the 1960s and '70s produced a robust economy and a demand for consumer products. The opportunities available to engineers in those years aren't available today — in part because all those engineers from the '60s and '70s are still around. "Now, we have to downsize in an economy that is certainly less than robust," she said.

Other areas around the country have been faced with similiar dilemmas before, where a heavily-relied-upon industry suddenly fell apart. The Quad City area of the upper Mississippi River valley, home to nearly 400,000 people in

Illinois and Iowa, once had a robust economy based on the manufacture of farm equipment. But when hard times hit that industry in the 1970s, the Quad Cities suffered losses in economic power and population. Census Bureau figures show that nearly one-fifth of the population left the area during the '80s, many of them baby boomers born between 1946 and 1965. "These are the people who are not only the producers of the community, but they're also a very large section of the consumers," Paul Elgatian, a labor market analyst with the Illinois Department of Employment Security, told the *Quad-City Times*. When the consumers left, the area's economy suffered overall.

More significant in economic terms were the jobs that replaced manufacturing as the Quad Cities tried to replace closed harvester and tractor plants with gambling boats and other tourist-related businesses. So, even though jobs may have been replaced one-for-one, the result was a "downsizing" of the entire area economy because a croupier doesn't make nearly the wage of a tool-and-dye maker and a waitress isn't nearly as well paid as an assembly-line worker.

*C*alifornia would like to avoid the problems faced by areas like the Quad Cities, and government officials are scrambling to find additional high-tech, high-wage jobs to help California's dismal economy. Announcements are coming from all sectors of the government and industry, emphasizing other technical areas that could absorb the aerospace job losses. Barry Sedlick, a manager with Southern California Edison and a principle co-author of a study on industry migration from the state, said that some newer industries like the electric vehicle, rail car and apparel industries could flourish in the Los Angeles area. At least once a week, the California Environmental Protection Agency announces new environmental technologies (such as hazardous waste management or air pollution control), requiring technical expertise that could be explored by private industry and encouraged by governmental policies. But the Economic Roundtable of Southern California found that aerospace workers wishing to work on rail cars would experience a loss of wages, the electric-car industry is too young to prove a viable alternative in the short run, and the relatively low-wage apparel industry is not a welcome replacement for high-wage aerospace jobs. Nor would aerospace workers automatically slide over to environmental technology. Most would have to be retrained, and probably take wage cuts.

As for the companies, they will simply tighten their budgets to survive and live with either smaller companies or move into different markets. Instead, it's the workers with particular skills who may not easily move into other jobs, and who may never again earn $18 an hour. California's economy will continue to suffer as these people spend less and less in the state, leading to less taxes and smaller state and local government budgets. Aerospace companies watch their bottom line get smaller, as state and local governments watch theirs diminish as well. But the most frustrated people may be the workers themselves. Not only do they not know where to turn, they don't know who to be angry with. Is it the federal government's fault for not preparing the country for a downsized defense industry, or California's fault for depening upon defense, or the educational system which for years painted aerospace as a lucrative industry. As former General Dynamics manager David Blanchard told "Frontline," "Who do you blame for the fact that peace broke out?"

THE JUSTICE SYSTEM

California has often been praised for the excellence of its state and local governments— relatively free of scandal, with high-quality civil servants, nationally respected governors (Hiram Johnson and Earl Warren among them) and a Legislature that at least once ranked first in a national survey. But perhaps the state's greatest gift to the nation was the leadership of its Supreme Court. Under a series of forceful chief justices — among them Phil Gibson, Roger Traynor and Donald Wright — the state's highest tribunal often led the way for the United States Supreme Court. The California Supreme Court built a reputation for activism and independence with decisions that struck down the death penalty (People v. Anderson, 1972), outlawed the state's system of financing public education (Serrano v. Priest, 1971) and invalidated an anti-fair housing initiative approved by the electorate (Mulkey v. Reitman, 1966).

The judiciary may be the most powerful of the three branches of state government because the Constitution is so detailed and because the Supreme Court has the power — which it had not been hesitant to use — to strike down acts of the Legislature or initiatives that conflict with the state and federal constitutions. The court also uses its power to void acts of the executive branch that violate either a statute or the constitution.

An activist Supreme Court has often been viewed as a second Legislature — more powerful than the first. Governor Ronald Reagan sought to reduce the activism of the court through his appointments, but one of the big disappointments of his eight years as governor was that his appointee for chief justice, Donald Wright, turned out to be another activist.

In 1977, Democratic Governor Edmund G. Brown Jr. had an opportunity to recast the court and by 1981 his appointees comprised a majority on the court. He appointed the court's first woman, Chief Justice Rose Elizabeth Bird; first black, the late Wiley W. Manuel; and first Latino, Cruz Reynoso. Bird was a highly controversial figure when she was appointed and throughout her tenure on the court. While there were many criticisms of the Bird court by conservatives, the most critical was the court's failure to allow any executions during her tenure as Chief Justice. (Polls indicate that over 80 percent of California citizens favored the death penalty.)

In November 1986, in an unprecedented election, three of the Brown-appointed liberals, Justices Bird, Reynoso and Joseph Grodin lost their confirmation elections. This enabled Governor George Deukmejian to appoint three new conservatives to the high court. These three combined with two previous appointments gave the court a conservative majority which it has retained to date.

Lower and appellate courts

The Supreme Court sits at the apex of the California judicial system. There are three lower levels — the justice and municipal courts, the superior courts, and the district courts of appeal. Members of the Supreme Court and the district courts of appeal are appointed by the governor subject to confirmation by the Commission on Judicial Appointments (consisting of the chief justice, the attorney general and one appeals-court justice). In recent years, the commission has called for public hearings on controversial appointees. Bird was approved by a 2-1 vote following a heated public debate. Incumbent judges' names appear on the ballot at the first general election following their appointment and again at the end of each 12-year term. If the incumbent receives a majority of "yes" votes for retention, he or she has another 12-year term.

• *Municipal and justice courts.* These local courts hear misdemeanor cases, preliminary hearings on some felony charges, small-claims actions and civil cases involving relatively small amounts of money (less than $25,000 in both municipal and justice courts).

• *Superior courts.* These countywide courts hear juvenile criminal cases, felonies, appeals from justice and municipal court decisions, and civil cases that cannot be tried in the municipal courts.

• *Courts of appeal.* These are divided into six districts (based in San Francisco, Los Angeles, Sacramento, San Diego, Fresno, and San Jose). Each division within each court contains three or four justices, with three justices normally sitting on each appeal. The court has jurisdiction over appeals from superior-court actions and decisions of quasi-judicial state boards.

• *The Supreme Court.* The state's highest court handles appeals from the district courts of appeal, although some cases can be taken directly from the trial court to the Supreme Court. In death-penalty cases, for example, appeals automatically go from the superior court to the Supreme Court. The high court also reviews orders of the Public Utilities Commission and has some appointive powers.

Judges of the municipal, justice and superior courts are elected by the people for six-year terms. Vacancies in justice court positions are filled by the county supervisors; the governor fills vacancies in the municipal and superior courts. On occasion, there is a wide-open race for a judgeship, but usually the post is filled by appointment and the incumbent retains the judgeship at the ensuing election.

A judge may be removed or otherwise disciplined by the Supreme Court — but only upon recommendation of the Commission on Judicial Performance, which is composed of five judges, two attorneys and two lay people. Judges are also subject to impeachment and recall, but the more common disciplinary procedure is through an investigation by the commission and action by the high court.

The state Judicial Council is a 21-member board charged with the overall administration of the court system. It is headed by the chief justice, who in turn appoints most of the members. The Administrative Office of the California Courts is the staff agency charged with carrying out the council's policies and conducting research for the council.

California uses the standard jury system. Grand juries (19 citizens in most counties, 23 in Los Angeles) investigate public agencies and have the power to hand down criminal indictments. However, the state Supreme Court ruled in 1978 that preliminary (probable-cause) hearings must be held, whether or not a suspect is indicted. Trial juries usually consist of 12 registered voters, but both sides in a case can agree to a smaller panel or waive a jury and submit the case to a judge. A unanimous vote is needed for acquittal or conviction in a criminal case.

CALIFORNIA'S COURT SYSTEM

U.S. SUPREME COURT

CALIFORNIA SUPREME COURT

Original jurisdiction; habeas corpus, mandamus, certiorari, prohibition

DISTRICT COURTS OF APPEAL

First District	Second District	Third District	Fourth District	Fifth District	Sixth District
San Francisco	Los Angeles	Sacramento	San Bernardino San Diego	Fresno	San Jose

Original jurisdiction; writs of mandamus, prohibition, habeas corpus, ceritorari

SUPERIOR COURTS
ONE IN EACH COUNTY

Original jurisdiction; Civil-amount in controversy exceeds $15,000, mandamus, habeas corpus, equitqable relief, probate, family law and juvenile court matters. Criminal-felonies.

MUNICIPAL COURTS

ONE IN EACH DISTRICT OF MORE THAN 40,000

Civil jurisdiction; amount in controversy, $15,000 or less. Criminal: lesser misdemeanors, preliminary hearings for felonies, infractions

MUNICIPAL COURTS

ONE IN EACH DISTRICT OF 40,000 OR LESS

Civil jurisdiction; amount in controversy, $15,000 or less. Criminal: misdemeanors, preliminary hearings for felonies, infractions

JUDICIAL COUNCIL

Makes rules on judicial procedure; surveys and expedites judicial business.

COMPOSITION:
Chief Justice
Fourteen judge appointees of chief justice
Four elected by State Bar
One Assembly
One Senate

COMMISSION ON JUDICIAL NOMINEE EVALUATION

Evaluates the Governor's prospective judge candidates.

COMPOSITION:
Nineteen elected by State Bar
Six appointed by governor

COMMISSION ON JUDICIAL PERFORMANCE

Confirms or rejects appointees of Governor to Supreme Court and Courts of Appeal

COMPOSITION:
Chief Justice
Attorney General
Senior Justice on Court of Appeals

COMMISSION ON JUDICIAL PERFORMANCE

Recommends to Supreme Court censure, removal or retirement of judges

COMPOSITION:
Five judges appointed by the Supreme Court
Two lawyers elected by State Bar
Two appointed by Governor

RECOMMENDATIONS, ADVICE CONFIRMATION

LINES OF APPEAL OR REVIEW

THE LUCAS COURT

Since Rose Bird's departure, the California Supreme Court has been less controversial, and less diverse

By Bob Egelko

Bob Egelko covers the state Supreme Court for the Associated Press.

Reprinted from *California Journal,* June 1994

People who have lost track of the state Supreme Court might not remember why California has no campaign funding limits for public financing of legislative elections this year. It isn't because of legislative or public opposition; in fact, 53 percent of the public voted for those changes in a 1988 initiative.

No, the reason is that the court extinguished that initiative in a 4-3 ruling last December, saying voters would have preferred the remnants of a rival measure that already had been gutted by federal courts.

Another question. "Why aren't Proposition 103 rate rollbacks moving ahead, six years after that initiative passed and three years after Insurance Commissioner John Garamendi adopted regulations and ordered hearings?"

Responsibility might be assigned to the state bureaucracy, the insurance industry or flaws in Proposition 103 itself. But the most immediate reason is that the court agreed a year ago to review the legality of the regulations, but hasn't scheduled a hearing yet or allowed Garamendi to implement rollbacks in the meantime.

Finally, why aren't new jails and courthouses being built in San Diego County with the money from a sales tax increase that was approved by a majority of the voters, under a financing system that the court seemed to have endorsed in 1982?

The reason is that a new court majority took another look in 1991 at the two-thirds vote required by Proposition 13 in 1978 for "special taxes," interpreted the requirement more broadly and struck down the San Diego measure.

Good or bad, these decisions, and the court that issued them, deserve more attention than they're getting.

Largely by upholding death sentences, the court headed by Chief Justice Malcolm Lucas for the last several years has managed to avoid the prominence and controversy that surrounded the Rose Bird court in the years leading up to the 1986 elections, when Bird and two colleagues were voted out of office. A return to a lower profile was probably healthy for the court and certainly welcomed by the justices. But the Lucas court is an important force in the state, and it's hard to understand its near-invisibility.

For example, although Justice Edward Panelli retired January 31, more than four months after announcing his plans, Governor Pete Wilson left the vacancy unfilled for months, with no criticism from his rivals. Meanwhile, the seventh seat at monthly oral arguments was occupied by a succession of appellate justices, including some Democrats.

In a year of obsession with crime and punishment, the court wasn't even mentioned during the primary elections for governor. The only candidates who seemed interested were two Democratic hopefuls for insurance commissioner, state Senator Art Torres and Assemblyman Burt Margolin; they joined some consumer groups this March in an unsuccessful request to the Deukmejian-appointed majority on the court to withdraw from an insurance case in which the former governor represented an insurance company.

The last time many legislators seem to have taken notice of the court was in 1991, when Lucas, in a ruling upholding a term-limits initiative, belittled the effect of a 38 percent cut in the Legislature's operating budget. Legislative committees rushed to propose a 38 percent reduction in the court's budget before cooler heads prevailed.

The court's funding could suffer if the governorship were won by a Democrat, who presumably would feel less affinity for the 6-1 majority of Republican appointees. But there isn't much a new governor could do about the current majority, which, barring personal tragedies or a major scandal, should be with us into the next century.

The three 1987 Deukmejian appointees who swung the court to the right — Justices John Arguelles, Marcus Kaufman and David Eagleson — all retired in less than four years, after becoming eligible for maximum retirement benefits. Their successors — Joyce Kennard, Armand Arabian and Marvin Baxter — are younger and have many years to go on the pension ladder, as does Wilson's first appointee, Ronald George, who succeeded the retiring Justice Allen Broussard in 1991.

Justice Stanley Mosk, at 81 a 30-year veteran and the only Democrat on the court, floated enough retirement rumors before the 1986 election to keep his potential opposition off balance, avoided the purge of his fellow liberals and has shown few signs of slowing down. He is the leading dissenter on the court, slightly ahead of Kennard, who established herself as the least predictable justice soon after her appointment in 1989.

As for Lucas, the 67-year-old chief justice remains the leader of the court's controlling bloc, though he no longer writes the most opinions, as he did for several years after his elevation by ex-law partner Deukmejian in 1987. He has a few years left before maximum pension eligibility, shows no obvious ill effects from a 1987 colon cancer operation, and hasn't dropped a hint about leaving.

Lucas also seems to have withstood the embarrassment of a *San Francisco Chronicle* account last November of his frequent out-of-state travels. The article disclosed that a Lloyds of London subsidiary, which had cases before Lucas' court, paid for two of his trips to overseas conferences, raising concerns about judicial ethics. Saying the trips were part of his job, Lucas asked for an investigation by the Commission on Judicial Performance, whose nine members include five judges appointed by the Supreme Court. The commission cleared him two months later, saying the unique nature of the chief justice's job should have dispelled any suggestion of illicit influence or appearance of impropriety.

Probably the harshest public evaluation of the court was another *Chronicle* article in November, concluding that the court had sunk into mediocrity since its trailblazing years of the 1950s to mid-'70s, based on interviews with scholars and assorted legal observers. Assessments like those are beyond the scope of the present article or the capability of its author, who wishes to observe only that objective standards are elusive, and it's probably more useful to examine the justices and their work in their own time.

The current court can be divided roughly into two phases. In the first three or four years, the court defined itself largely by deciding how far to go in discarding or narrowing the doctrines of the Bird court and its predecessors. Conservatives were firmly in control, but the presence of Mosk, Broussard, and later Kennard kept debate brisk and dissents relatively frequent.

Some of the biggest plums fell quickly. In 1987 the court, under the surprising authorship of Mosk, ruled that a death sentence could be imposed without proof of intent to kill, overturning the key decision in the Bird court's death-penalty reversals. The next year, majorities led by Lucas barred suits by third parties against insurance companies for mishandling or delaying claims — overruling a 1979 decision detested by insurers — and severely limited damages for wrongful firings.

As expected, the court also started giving generous readings to initiatives that the Bird court had interpreted more narrowly. The 1991 ruling in the San Diego County case, strengthening Proposition 13's clout against local taxes, was the culmination of a trend of several years. Prosecutors won longer sentences and broader rules on confessions under a 1982 crime initiative known as the Victims' Bill of Rights. The court's sympathetic view of initiatives may have saved consumer-sponsored Proposition 103 in 1989 when the justices decided to rewrite rather than discard its rollback of insurance rates.

In civil rights, where previous courts had expanded the reach of anti-discrimination laws, the Lucas court displayed its empathy for businesses and its distrust of regulatory agencies in a series of rulings by Panelli, starting in 1987, that trimmed the powers of the state Fair Employment and Housing Commission. In 1990 the court barred suits against businesses for discriminating against the poor but said it would allow other claims of arbitrary bias recognized by the Bird court. Lower courts have had trouble deciphering that ruling, and it's likely to be refined in a future case.

The first phase contained a few surprises — the rejection of a "sub-minimum" wage for work-ers receiving tips, the upholding of a one-house legislative veto of Deukmejian's nomination of Dan Lungren as state treasurer — and one outright stunner: Over the repeated dissents of Lucas and Panelli, the remaining appointees of anti-abortion Governor Deukmejian joined their colleagues in refusing to reconsider a Bird court ruling continuing state funding for Medi-Cal abortions.

Attempts to curtail the funding were later dropped by Wilson, but the abortion issue may soon be back before the court in the form of a never-enforced state law requiring parental consent or a judge's approval for an unmarried minor's abortion. The court finally addressed the underlying privacy issue this January in a ruling upholding drug testing of college athletes; Lucas' majority opinion, a masterpiece of ambiguity, contained much talk of core values and balancing tests, but few clues about the court's approach to abortion or other privacy disputes.

The court entered its second phase around 1991, when the majority was solidified by the appointment of George, a bright and ambitious former state death-penalty lawyer, to succeed Broussard — Jerry Brown's last remaining appointee. Its task of culling the casebooks for undesirable precedents largely complete, the court enjoyed a friendly legal landscape and political security, and could set its own agenda.

At times, this included bursts of activism usually associated with more liberal courts. After a legislative attempt to declare surrogate-motherhood contracts legal and regulate them was vetoed by Wilson, the court declared one type of surrogacy legal without regulation last year. Dismissing suggestions that a contract to bear another's child for pay exploited poor women, Panelli's opinion coolly observed that poverty often induces women to take bad jobs. Kennard, dissenting from the all-male majority, said the court was devaluing the role of the birth mother.

More often, the court has stayed true to its creed of judicial restraint, deferring to the decisions of legislators, voters and trial judges. But the court has encountered some unforeseen problems in the last few years, often as the consequences of its own earlier decisions.

First and foremost was the death penalty, the downfall of the Bird court and the top priority of the Lucas court. The repeal of the intent-to-kill requirement cleared the way for a dramatic turnaround of the affirmance rate — from 6 percent under Bird to more than 90 percent in the last four years, the highest in the nation. Critical of the previous court's second-guessing of trial judges, the new majority relied on the doctrine of "harmless error," regularly concluding that mistaken rulings could not have influenced the jury's death verdict. The concept was sometimes carried to great lengths, excusing a judge's improper refusal to let a murderer tell jurors why he deserved to live, and another judge's erroneous decision to allow evidence of a gruesome wine-bottle rape.

The court also tore into the case backlog, deciding 56 capital appeals in a single year, 12 fewer than the Bird court had resolved in seven years. To promote efficiency and discourage repeated appeals, the court adopted time limits and other procedural restrictions, in a 1992 ruling modeled on a U.S. Supreme Court decision.

But the backlog refused to disappear, and instead changed shape: The number of Death Row inmates without lawyers rose above 100, and the average waiting period for a lawyer reached three years, as a combination of limited pay and bleak prospects discouraged experienced attorneys from accepting capital appeals. That meant cases were taking longer to reach the court, and potential new grounds for future appeals were being created. Meanwhile, the court's efforts to dismiss new claims on procedural grounds without a hearing were meeting a chilly reception when the cases arrived before federal judges, increasing the likelihood that death sentences would be reversed and cases returned to state courts for new trials.

The length and arduousness of capital cases also took time away from civil cases, held down the court's statistical output and may have spurred some justices toward retirement. A commission appointed by Lucas in 1987 had recommended shifting some of the death-penalty workload to state appeals courts, but Lucas never endorsed the idea and it's scarcely been mentioned since.

Another area that has proven more complicated than it first appeared is torts, the broad field of liability for physical, mental and financial injuries. Decisions of the early years seemed to yield some simple rules. Tort suits were not to be the primary instrument of public protection or social policy; thus, foot-dragging by insurers was to be deterred by regulators, not by private lawsuits, and crime was to be controlled by police and lawmakers, not by victims' damage suits against landowners for faulty security. Another maxim was that firm lines had to be drawn around liability, at the price of occasional harshness to individuals. So a mother who heard neighbors scream, and ran outside to see her child lying in the street, couldn't sue a hit-and-run driver for emotional distress because she didn't see the accident. And someone who saw a lover die in a car crash caused by a drunken driver couldn't sue unless the couple was married.

This approach has the advantage of clarity and doesn't have to sacrifice an understanding of human problems. One of the court's most acclaimed and influential rulings was a 1990 case balancing the rights of patients and the interests of medical researchers. A man sued doctors after an organ, removed during a life-saving operation, was tested and found to contain a cell pattern that was a potential source of new medical products. The court rejected the patient's claim of a violation of property rights, which could have entitled him to a share of the profits; but Panelli's majority opinion let him sue the doctor on more limited grounds, for failing to inform the patient of the research plans or obtain his consent. The ruling provided guidance to doctors and patients, left research unimpeded and discouraged the exploitation of unknowing patients.

But not all problems can be resolved so neatly. The court's tendency to create rigid categories, and its inclination to limit damage suits, have led it at times to try to pound square pegs into round holes. A glaring example involved assumption of risk, the doctrine that denies all damages to a person who engages in a dangerous activity and is injured by someone else's negligence. Most state courts have treated the concept as outdated since a 1975 state Supreme Court ruling that allowed damages when both parties were negligent, with the award reduced by the proportion of the victim's fault. But the Lucas court signaled in 1990 that it might revive the prohibition on damages, and granted review of about a dozen cases. Two years later, the court produced a fragmented and bewildering ruling.

In the case of a woman injured during a company football game, three justices, led by George, said sports participants had no duty to act carefully, and could be sued only for reckless or intentional harm. Three others, led by Kennard, said a suit should be allowed only if injuries resulted from activities that were more dangerous than the victim anticipated. The seventh justice, Mosk, said assumption of risk was outmoded, but agreed with George that no duty had been breached. Even the court couldn't figure out which of those standards to apply to the next case that raised the issue. The result, apparently, was that the approach of letting juries weigh the fault of each side had been discarded for dangerous activities, without any clearly defined policy to put in its place.

Further trouble lay ahead in a more significant case, involving suits for fear of disease caused by pollution. In the case of Salinas-area residents who learned their water wells had been contaminated with carcinogens, lower courts found their fears of cancer reasonable and awarded damages against the polluting company. But the Supreme Court, urged by businesses to prohibit all such suits and leery of "speculative fears," devised a new rule last December; In normal cases, damages would be awarded only if plaintiffs could prove they were more likely than not to become ill. But apparently unwilling to throw the Salinas residents out of court, the majority, led by Baxter, created an alternate test: They would have to prove only a significant risk of disease, because the polluter (according to the court) had disregarded a known risk of harm. The decision left the many interested parties on both sides neither satisfied nor enlightened. The new standards seemed arbitrary and the boundary lines murky. Underlying the decision may have been the court's unstated view that fears, like other emotions, are too intangible to be trusted as the basis of a lawsuit.

A similar approach outside the tort field resulted in perhaps the court's most awkward ruling in recent years — the December 1993 decision denying enforcement of Proposition 68, a 1988 campaign finance initiative.

Voters approved two political reform measures on the same ballot. Proposition 68, which included contribution limits as well as partial public financing for legislative candidates who limited their spending, got 53 percent of the vote. Proposition 73, which contained a different system of contribution limits and several other provisions, including a ban on public financing, got 58 percent. The state Constitution says the ballot measure with the most votes

even if they'd known in advance that the rest of the measure was invalid. What was left of Proposition 73 was still a competing regulatory scheme, and there was no room for Proposition 68, the court said.

The result was cheered by legislators and major contributors, but was hard to square with the court's professed reverence for the people's will. Two initiatives, both approved by a majority of the voters, had added up to zero reform. The ruling didn't even end the case; Proposition 73's legislative authors were soon back before the justices, asking for a new ruling that would rewrite their measure and cure its legal flaws.

The last few years have shown some weaknesses in the Lucas court, but the court is not without its strengths. It retains the support of much of the bench and bar, quickly mobilized behind Lucas when his travels came under scrutiny. It is also accepted by most of the public, which handily approved the current justices when they've appeared on the ballot, and is likely to do so again this fall. Despite a decline in the number of rulings, due largely to the increase in death penalty cases, the court is as hard-working as any of its predecessors. Lucas takes his leadership role seriously and has appointed productive task forces on racial and gender bias, technology, and the future of the court system. Mosk has been one of the nation's highest-regarded state judges for many years; the lesser-known Kennard and George appear to be extremely capable jurists with much untapped potential.

But the court, like a medieval royal family,

prevails, but an appeals court, following some earlier appellate rulings, decided to allow enforcement of the parts of Proposition 68 that didn't conflict with Proposition 73. The Supreme Court disagreed and announced a new rule in 1990: When two ballot measure contain competing regulatory schemes, the measure with fewer voters is entirely unenforceable.

However, federal courts were already in the process of dismantling Proposition 73, and soon ruled that its core provision, the contribution limits, unconstitutionally favored incumbents. Proposition 68 had no such defect, so its sponsor, Common Cause, asked the state Supreme Court to revive the measure, since its rival had been effectively nullified. But the Supreme Court refused, and declared that Proposition 73 wasn't entirely dead; one previously obscure provision, broadening an existing ban on publicly financed mass political mailings, was unaffected by the federal rulings and was actually part of the essential purpose of the initiative, said the four-member majority. Lucas' opinion said voters would have passed that provision by itself,

suffers from inbreeding. For 12 years, two governors with a common agenda have promoted a succession of mostly like-minded justices from the appellate courts, with similar backgrounds as business or government lawyers, while stocking the lower courts with ex-prosecutors. When the high court justices sit around the conference table, there are no former poverty lawyers, civil-rights lawyers, labor lawyers, public defenders or academics, and probably few who have ever represented or have ever been, a poor person. That's not a formula for healthy debate. When the court hits a dead end in its thinking, it needs new ideas and new perspectives to find a way out.

Oddly enough, a possible prototype for change is sitting in the governor's office. When Wilson was a U.S. senator recommending candidates for federal judgeships, his picks were fairly diverse, sexually, racially, professionally and even ideologically. His appointments as governor have fit a different mold, but whoever is elected this November could strengthen the court by following Senator Wilson's model.

CRAIG RILEY SCHINDLER 92

The High Cost of Death

By Don Babwin

O n Easter morning, April 19th, newspapers all over the country were plastered with headlines about a judge's order to stay the execution of condemned murderer Robert Alton Harris — the first person slated to die in California's gas chamber in 25 years. It was only the latest delay in a case that already had bounced around the courts for nearly 14 years, and angry state officials reacted by saying they would appeal the stay immediately — as in Easter Sunday — to a federal court. And, the stories indicated, the losers in that appeal would take their case to the U.S. Supreme Court the very next day.

Translation: The financial tab on a case that had cost millions of dollars was going to climb at least a little higher, and could have gone a lot higher had the federal high court not put an end to the process. Harris died in San Quentin's gas chamber just after 6 a.m. on Tuesday, April 21st, his last appeal having been emphatically rejected by the Court less than an hour earlier.

To be sure, when talking about the ultimate punishment, there are more important aspects to consider than money. But with more than 300 residents of San Quentin's Death Row all waiting in the wings with their own lengthy and costly appeals, the death penalty represents a major financial strain on an already strapped state budget. Opponents of the death penalty say to execute the prisoners already on death row would cost $1 billion. Ironically, while proponents of the death penalty say much of that money finances unnecessary and frivolous

Don Babwin is a reporter for The Press-Enterprise *of Riverside.*

appeals, opponents argue that recent developments in the appellate process will mean a shortage of cash needed to finance these cases.

Capital cases are rarely quick and never cheap. For example, while Harris' long legal odyssey generated headlines, the longest resident of death row, Andrew Edward Robertson, is still well back in the appellate pipeline — at the point Harris occupied a decade ago. The cases, which are meticulously researched, may take years to prepare. Just getting to trial may take years. Warren James Bland, the suspected murderer of a 7-year-old South Pasadena girl, has been sitting in county jail for more than five years. His trial in Riverside has yet to begin.

The trials themselves are expensive. In Riverside County, for example, police recently arrested William Suff, a man suspected of killing prostitutes and drug users. It is a good bet that the trial will include a parade of experts dealing with everything from DNA (did Suff rape the women?) to child abuse to answer questions about Suff's past. One county official estimated the case may cost as much as $5 million to $10 million. A complicated murder case might include the testimony of psychiatrists, toxicologists and pathologists. If one side calls such a witness, it is a safe bet the other side is going to call its own "expert" to the witness stand. All of these witnesses cost money.

But how much money is not easy to determine. Defense costs, for example, are confidential until a case becomes final — in other words, until the sentence is carried out. Thus, prosecutors have no way to review defense costs for a single resident of Death Row. The only time prosecutors were able to find out defense costs involved an inmate, Joselito Cinco, who hanged himself a few months after being sentenced to death for murdering two San Diego police officers.

Not counting what Cinco's two attorneys charged San Diego County to defend him, the bill was more than a half-million dollars, according to Richard Neely, the San Diego County assistant district attorney who prosecuted the case. Add what the defense attorneys charged, and the cost to defend Cinco easily reached $1 million, Neely said. That figure does not include what the district attorney's office spent to prosecute Cinco. Neely could not estimate how many hours he spent on the case but said for the eight months it took to try the case, prosecuting Cinco was his job.

At the time Cinco killed himself, his case was in the earliest stage of the appellate process. Legal experts say the appeals are much more expensive than the initial trial. In the Harris case, for example, the attorney general's office spent $750,000 and devoted some 6000 attorney hours to the appeals, according to David Puglia, a spokesman for the attorney general's office.

Capital cases can devastate local economies. "We could not fund one at this point," said Don Hemphill, the auditor of Sierra County. "We might have to cut police, very possibly, and other services."

Hemphill said the county had several capital cases in the 1980s and managed to pay for them. He said the state picked up the bulk of the $500,000 to $700,000 it costs to prosecute the cases, with the county's share 10 percent of that. To a county of 3500 permanent residents, $50,000 to $70,000 is a lot of money, he said.

"The only thing that saved us was the economy was well," Hemphill said. Like other counties throughout the state, the economic picture has changed for the worse in recent years.

Until recently, counties were reimbursed by the state for defense costs other than attorneys' fees, with the cost of experts and tests being paid for through what is called "987.9 funding" from the state. But that source of money is gone.

In Siskiyou County a few years ago, the fund provided a $266,000 reimbursement from the state, according to Dave Elledge, the county's auditor-controller. For a county with a general fund budget of about $23 million, said Elledge, "That's a lot of money."

"I don't know how we would come up with that," Elledge said. As in Sierra County, Elledge said such a case without special funding from the state would likely mean pink slips for some county employees.

As for the state, the death penalty is a financial drain. In 1989 *The Sacramento Bee* reported that the state could save $90 million a year by abolishing the death penalty. Critics such as Semel say there is no reason to believe that figure would not be even greater today. Considering that it costs the state $24,600-a-year to house a prisoner in San Quentin, according to the state's Department of Corrections, a 40-year stay costs $984,000. Pat Clark of the anti-death penalty group, Death Penalty Focus, said studies show a capital case costs anywhere from $1.8 million to $45 million.

But proponents of the death penalty counter that costs are high because convicted death-row inmates file frivolous, repetitive claims in federal court. These, said David Puglia, drive costs up. Besides, said Puglia, the primary goal of the death penalty has never been to save money. "The death penalty is appropriate for the crimes that it was put on the books to cover," he said. "That is the reason for the death penalty."

There is growing concern among defense attorneys that contrary to the popular perception that too much money is spent on death penalty appeals, the opposite is true. Defense attorneys say they are being priced out of the appellate process and can no longer afford to take the cases.

What is happening, say attorneys, is that the state Supreme Court is refusing to reimburse them for what they say are absolutely necessary expenses. In 1990 the Supreme Court adopted "payment guidelines" outlining how much it would pay for various phases of capital-case appeals. For example, attorneys are paid $75 an hour. While the Court maintains that the rate is the highest in the country, it is still considerably below the $200-$300 hourly rate attorneys charge paying clients. And according to a February 1992 article in *The Sacramento Bee*, an appeal should take between 815 and 1830 hours per case.

The Court also detailed the maximum rates it would allow for investigators, psychiatrists, paralegals and others who might assist in the appeals. Asaro said the rate of $125 an hour for a psychiatrist is unrealistic. "A psychiatrist can bill $300 to $350 an hour," she said. That leaves attorneys in the position of having to pay the fees out of their own pockets.

"You're finding lawyers personally in debt, or refusing to take the cases," said Semel. Asaro said she has spent "thousands of dollars" of her own money on death-penalty cases. Her law partner, Sanford Rosen, was told that a $12,297 bill he submitted for paralegal services was disallowed under the guidelines, according to the *Bee*. Financially, no law firm can handle more than two death penalty

DEATH continued on page 35

THE PRISON DILEMMA

California locks up more and more felons, so why don't we feel safer?

By Danielle Starkey and Vic Pollard

Reprinted from *California Journal*, April 1994

Adrian Raine's throat was slashed by a robber a few years ago. "I was furious. I was boiling. I wanted this guy put away forever,"Raine said recently.

But as a criminologist at the University of Southern California, Raine said he also recognized that locking up the robber and throwing away the key were not likely to reduce his chances of getting mugged in the future.

That Raine was mugged at all was, statistically speaking, a rare event. Despite the public's fear about crime, and the perception that it's getting worse, the state's overall crime rate has actually dropped since the peak year of 1980 in all except the violent-crime category. Much of the increase in violent crime is due to a reporting change because of legislation in 1986 that reclassified domestic violence from a misdemeanor to a felony.

Still, while statistics suggest that we should feel safer, few of us do. California's prison population has tripled since 1984, and the state spent more than $13 billion last year on its criminal justice system, which includes law enforcement, prosecution, probation, jails and prisons. Yet many people feel we're not doing enough, or the right things, to make a difference. Even if our chances of being murdered are about the same as dying of AIDS (.1 per 100,000), it's impossible to ignore, for example, that violent crime among juveniles is increasing at an alarming rate: The percentage of youths in the California Youth Authority for homicide went from 6.8 percent in 1987 to 12.1 percent in 1991.

But part of the problem is one of perception: News reports about a recent spate of particularly vicious, senseless crimes — most notably, the kidnap-murder of 12-year-old Polly Klaas — has made public safety a top political issue. Polls show that crime and violence have replaced the economy as the number-one concern among voters, resulting in a truckload of new legislation to crack down on criminals. California is one of at least 23 states considering proposals to sharply stiffen penalties for repeat offenders, usually labeled "three strikes and you're out." These measures differ in detail, but most are designed to impose longer sentences on people who have shown a propensity to commit repeated violent or serious offenses.

The new wave of anti-crime sentiment comes after more than a decade of increasingly stiffer penalties for many crimes. That has left much of the nation, especially California, with overcrowded prisons that consume an ever-growing share of scarce taxpayer dollars. Despite growing public fear and anger about crime, the question remains: Will locking up more criminals really make the streets safer?

Traditionally, the debate has been between two philosophies about human nature. There are those who say crime is a product of poverty, drugs or an abusive upbringing, and that vocational and educational programs could help turn around the lives of most offenders. And there are those who say that criminals are deviants who should be put away.

The debate is not new. In the 1920s and '30s, which included the bank-robbing heyday of Bonnie and Clyde, politicians were confronted with the same kind of demand for harsher penalties, said University of Minnesota law professor Michael Tonry. They reacted much the same way, passing harsh laws to crack down on what were then called "habitual offenders." But as prisons filled with increasingly elderly inmates like Robert Stroud, the famed "Bird Man of Alcatraz," a backlash set in during the 1950s and '60s. Rehabilitation advocates gained the upper hand, the death penalty became more controversial, and some states even granted wholesale pardons, Tonry said. The pendulum began swinging back the other way in the 1970s, as California and other states revived specific sentences for most crimes.

Back under California's old, indeterminate sentencing law (enacted in 1918), felons were sentenced to an open-ended term, such as five-years-to-life. Their actual release date was determined on a case-by-case basis by a state body called the Adult Authority, which answered to no one and based its decisions on the inmates's crime and prison behavior.

"Under the indeterminate sentencing law, when you went to prison, you weren't quite sure when you were going to get out," said Bernie Orozco, a senior fiscal and policy analyst with the Legislative Analyst's Office. Further, there was a strong incentive to "be good" once you got out that doesn't exist today.

"It was a system to make sure that you were rehabilitated," said Orozco. "If by chance you did get out, and you acted up or had another incident, they could send you back [to prison] for the rest of your life."

The incentive apparently was effective. In 1975 only 11 percent of parolees were returned to prison for parole violations or for committing new crimes, according to the Little Hoover Commission, a watchdog agency of the executive branch of state government. By 1990, however, almost 80 percent of those released on parole were returned to prison for committing new crimes or violating the conditions of parole, although that rate has dropped to about 60 percent since then because the Department of Corrections has adopted a new policy of not sending back to prison many who violated terms of their parole.

The rapid rise in recidivism came in part as a result of the Determinate Sentencing Act of 1977, which essentially caused parole to fall by the wayside, and which itself grew out of complaints that indeterminate sentencing was subjective and racist. Even the California Supreme Court upheld a 1975 case that found that the Adult Authority didn't have standardized guidelines.

The act, which initially created finite sentences for each offense based on an average of time currently served for the crime, also "explicitly abandoned the long-standing purpose of prison as rehabilitation and instead established punishment as the state goal," according to a January 1994 report by the Little Hoover Commission — "Putting Violence

Behind Bars: Redefining the Role of California's Prisons."

Since its enactment, piecemeal revisions of the law — usually following on the heels of a sensational crime — have resulted in a hodgepodge of sentencing requirements that one legal expert said "resembles the best offering of those who author bureaucratic memoranda, income tax forms, insurance policies or instructions for the assembly of packaged toys."

The repercussions of the law and its revisions have been extraordinary, and to some degree, unanticipated. "Every time there was a new crime that got media attention," sentencing requirements changed, said Jeannine English, executive director of the Little Hoover Commission. "There are people in prison for white-collar crimes serving sentences that are longer than for second-degree murderers, and burglary gets a longer sentence than taking corrosive acid and throwing it in someone's face."

In addition, inmates' release is no longer contingent on being able to show a means of support, or an evaluation of a successful transition back into society. For example, in the past year, 1022 inmates were released on parole from Pelican Bay, where most of the state's worst criminals are housed. Of these, 280 were released from the infamous "hole," or super-maximum security unit, where there are no efforts made to provide counseling, training or an education, and where inmates spend 22.5 hours per day in their cells.

"They're given $200 and dropped off at the Crescent City bus station," said English, of the Hoover Commission. One of these inmates took his cash, boarded a bus for the Bay Area and, within a month, had assaulted and raped a woman.

Another infamous parolee was multiple kidnapper Richard Allen Davis, charged in Polly Klaas's death. "All of the people who had worked with Richard Allen Davis, all of the people who knew him, *knew* he was going to continue his life of violence," said English. But he had served his time, so out he went.

"Our recommendation is that we keep violent offenders

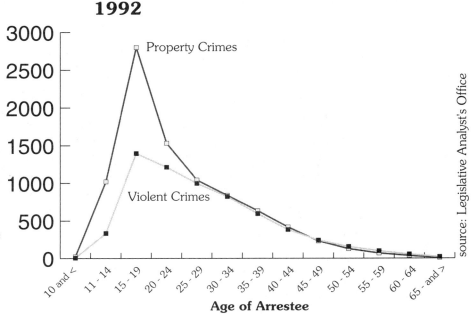

Felony Arrests Highest Among The Young[a]
1992

- Felony crime arrest rates peak in the 15- to 19-year-old age group.

- About half of all persons arrested in California in 1992 were between the ages of 11 and 24. This group, however, makes up only about 20 percent of the state's total population.

[a]Rate per 100,000 age-eligible population

Property Crimes

Violent Crimes

Age of Arrestee

source: Legislative Analyst's Office

in prison until we're sure they're not going to be a threat, and to use other forms of punishment for non-violent offenders," said English. "That would be more cost-effective, and better for public safety, and create an opportunity to rehabilitate some of the non-violent offenders we deem could be rehabilitated."

In addition to giving indefinite sentences for violent criminals and habitual offenders, and restricting their ability to earn reduced sentence time, the Little Hoover Commission recommends lengthening the time beyond the present limitation of one year that a parolee can be returned to prison for a violent crime.

Yet lawmakers, and the public, remain enamoured of the three-strikes bills that would in fact incapacitate those who've committed crimes, but also would represent a multi-billion dollar investment in the back-end — and most expensive portion — of the state's criminal justice system. Assemblyman Phil Isenberg, a Sacramento Democrat, was one of the few legislators to try to stick out his hand to stop the locomotive, when he urged a "no" vote on the three-strikes bills before the Assembly. He said that, since he was elected in 1982, the prison population has gone from 28,000 to 120,000, and 10 prisons have been built, yet the public feels less secure than ever.

"You would think that if security is the goal, someone would step back and say, 'Wait a minute, if we tried higher penalties, greater enhancements, building more prisons, putting more people away and [we] still don't feel safe, then what's the answer?' Well, how about higher penalties, putting more people away, building more prisons, spending more... I mean, even a casual observer of the scene would say there's something screwy," Isenberg said.

Isenberg said one of the Legislature's goals should be to ensure that space in prison is available for violent offenders. Currently, 43 percent of all people in state prisons are there for violent crimes, and 57 percent are in for non-violent crimes. That's largely because local decision-makers naturally choose the least costly sentencing option from their perspective, and prison is free for them.

"Are we willing to say if we move non-violent people out of state prison that we ought to create alternative punishments for them? Hell no, we're not willing to say that. Why? Well, because somebody may put out an attack piece of mail that says you're soft on crime," Isenberg told his Assembly colleagues.

Criminal-justice experts are watching the "lock 'em up" frenzy with reactions ranging from sad bemusement to alarm. Decades of research have failed to turn up any solid evidence that longer sentences have been a significant deterrent on crime, RAND researcher Peter Greenwood told state senators considering the "three strikes" bills. Greenwood said certain offenses such as drunk driving may drop temporarily after penalties are stiffened due to a "shock" effect. "But whatever deterrent effect it has goes away in a year or two," he said.

Tonry said the chief reason is that most crimes, particularly violent crimes, are impulsive acts committed by people who don't stop to think about the consequences. Tonry and other experts also point out that the trend toward ever-longer mandatory sentences ignores the fact that the vast majority of crimes are committed by young men between the ages of

15 and 24 (see graph, page 33).

Except for individuals with serious mental illness, "There's huge amounts of evidence that the fires that burn inside people that cause them to commit violent crimes begin to burn out by the time they get to their 40s," Tonry said. "If you lock people up until they're in their 50s and 60s, all you're getting out of it is some temporary emotional satisfaction."

Increasing attention is also being paid to biological factors that appear to predispose people to violence, such as head injuries and birth complications, although the conclusions are still speculative and controversial.

So how can the state fashion a corrections policy that keeps violent offenders off the streets and does not eat up money needed for other public programs? There are some examples of systems that work well, experts say. Minnesota and Delaware are credited with creating some of the best models in the 1980s. They rejected both mandatory sentences for all crimes and indeterminate sentences, in which parole decisions are usually made on a case-by-case basis by gubernatorial appointees. Instead, they set up independent agencies that established sentencing guidelines that take into account a wide variety of factors in each individual case, such as the seriousness of the crime and the likelihood of repeat offenses.

Since Delaware's guidelines went into effect in 1987, it has seen a marked increase in incarceration for violent crimes, while incarceration for non-violent offenses has dropped by almost half and its prison population has even declined slightly, according to the National Conference of State Legislatures. Experts caution that such a system must be coupled with an effective probation and parole supervision system, programs that have been increasingly starved for money in California in recent years. They also warn against adopting a system that is too complicated to administer fairly, the chief complaint about the controversial guidelines of the federal judicial system.

California's Legislative Analyst's Office recommended last year in its booklet, "Making Government Make Sense," that the state work more closely with local governments to decide how to best utilize each other's resources. "The way it's set up now, they're each trying to shunt off workloads on each other," said Orozco. In other words, since local governments can send people to prison at no charge, that's exactly what they choose to do, even though it costs more to taxpayers.

"The [local governments] should determine the length of the sentence, and they should pay for the service" through a revenue-redistribution plan, said Craig Cornett, director of criminal justice and state administration for the LAO. "We think that changes the fiscal incentives in a really positive way, and among other things encourages them to do more at the front end for prevention in order to prevent that back end cost."

In addition, Cornett said, a blue-ribbon commission convened in 1990 on inmate population management produced a comprehensive, balanced study that has largely been ignored.

"The key conclusion they had was that the system is out of balance, which we think is completely true," Cornett said. "We have too many resources at the back end, and not enough at the middle or at the beginning. We especially

Crime Rate Remains Stable Despite Sharp Increase in Imprisonment[a]
1971 Through 1992

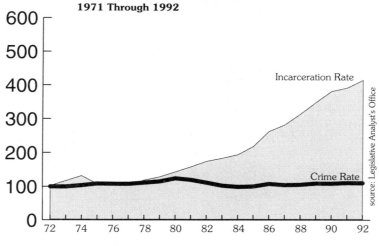

- California's incarceration rate has increased almost 300 percent since 1971 while the crime rate remained relatively flat (it increased about 11 percent).

- Some reasearchers argue that this situation should be expected because they believe that incarcerating more people for a longer period of time has no impact on the crime rate. Others disagree and argue that the crime rate would have increased significantly if the rate of imprisonment had not increased so significantly.

source: Legislative Analyst's Office

[a] Change in rates per 100,000 population, indexed to 1972

don't have enough at the front end to prevent people from becoming defendants or to deal with them when they first enter the system, but we put a lot of resources in the back end to warehouse people in state prison after they've committed the crime."

Nevertheless, it's likely that's exactly where money is going to go, given the momentum of the "three strikes" solution. Governor Pete Wilson's administration, in what it acknowledged is a conservative estimate, predicted recently that the proposed "three strikes" initiative would require construction of 20 new prisons by the turn of the century — in addition to the 12 new facilities expected to be needed under current sentencing laws. They would cost $2 billion a year to operate. Prison operating costs would continue to increase for the first 30 years under the program, maxing out at $5.7 billion a year by 2027.

These numbers didn't seem to deter lawmakers, however; during the first week of March, a bill identical to the "three strikes" initiative breezed out of the Legislature and was signed by Governor Wilson. Alternative bills, designed to address other problems as well as get tough on violent criminals, stalled. During the second week of March, proponents of the "three strikes" initiative turned in signatures to get their measure on the ballot. 🏛

DEATH continued from page 31

appeals, said Asaro. Within the guidelines the Court says it "will provide reasons in writing for fee disallowances of $1000 or more, and expense disallowances of $500 or more."

But, Asaro said, "The reality is they don't need a reason. The only explanation is that [the request for reimbursement] exceeds the guidelines."

Court spokeswoman Lynn Holton said the guidelines were adopted after "extensive Court review and comment from the State Bar, local bars, defense attorneys and the California Appellate Project." Further, she said in a prepared statement read by another Court official, "The Supreme Court follows a careful review process when it evaluates expense claims of court-appointed counsel in capital appeals. Each claim is thoroughly reviewed and nothing is done arbitrarily."

Another development that has defense attorneys worried is the decision by the state Supreme Court to take from the California Appellate Project (CAP) the job of recruiting attorneys to handle the appeals in death-penalty cases. CAP, which had done the recruiting and screening of attorneys, now serves solely as an adviser to the court. The Court said it made its decision because of the growing number of condemned prisoners who were without attorneys. According to an article in the March 25th edition of the legal newspaper, the *Daily Journal*, Associate Justice Ronald George said the Court had to step in because CAP has been "unsuccessful in bringing down the backlog." Since January 1991, George said, the number of condemned prisoners has increased by about 60.

Defense attorneys fear the result will be less-qualified attorneys assigned to death-penalty cases. And George told the *Daily Journal*, "It's our firm intention and desire not to lower the standards."

But attorneys say that has already happened. "The first person they picked was somebody without any complex criminal litigation or appellate experience," said John Cotsirillos, a San Diego attorney who is handling the appeal of convicted murderer Jackson Daniels of Riverside.

The Court's first selection was former Chief Deputy State Public Defender Matthew Newman. According to the *Daily Journal*, Newman "lacks experience in either death penalty or homicide cases..."

Cotsirillos said the guidelines are geared toward experienced attorneys, not attorneys who have never handled complicated appeals. Thus, it is more likely that guidelines might be exceeded, some critics say.

The cost of bringing a convicted felon from crime scene to gas chamber is but one aspect in the growing debate over use of the death penalty. Polls continue to show that a majority of Californians support the death penalty, and reminders about the ultimate cost of such cases are not likely to erode much of that support. But those reminders are instructive, for they show that the price of the ultimate penalty remains high. 🏛

THE LEGISLATURE

California's Legislature is not much different from Congress and legislative bodies in other states in overall power and structure. It is, simply stated, the policy-making arm of government, restricted only by the federal and state constitutions and the governor's veto. Like Congress, it can also conduct investigations into almost any issue of public concern and impeach public officials. The Senate must ratify top-level, non-judicial appointments of the governor, while both houses have the opportunity to reject the executive's nominations for any vacancy among the state's constitiutional offices. It also can ratify amendments to the United States Constitution. In recent years, there has been a trend toward the Legislature's appropriating for itself some of the appointive power traditionally given to the executive. Thus, it is not uncommon now to have a commission consist of both gubernatorial and legislative appointees.

Seats in both the 40-member Senate and 80-member Assembly are apportioned on the basis of population. (Until 1966, the Senate was apportioned by geography, like the United States Senate.) Assembly members serve two-year terms; Senate terms are for four years, with half the terms expiring every two years. Under the provisions of Prop. 140 of November 1990, term limits are now imposed on state legislators (3 terms, 6 years in the Assembly; 2 terms, 8 years in the Senate). The Senate and Assembly are organized differently, with power diffused in a committee of the upper house but centered in the office of speaker in the Assembly.

The Senate

The lieutenant governor is the president of the Senate, but this official has virtually no power. The lieutenant governor is entitled to cast a vote to break a 20-20 tie, but this situation almost never develops. If the Senate can be said to have a single leader it is the president pro tempore, who is elected by a simple majority of his colleagues. The pro tem is charged with overall administration of the house, but the real power — committee appointments and assignment of bills to committee — rests with the five-member Rules Committee. The president pro tempore is chairman, and the other four seats are traditionally divided between the two major parties. Between 1969 and 1975, there was an almost-constant battle for the leadership post between two factions sometimes referred to as the Old Guard and the Young Turks. However, in recent years the divisions in the Senate have tended to be along party lines. There has been stability in leadership, at least among Democrats, since 1980 when David Roberti became president pro tempore.

Aside from the Rules Committee, the two most important panels in the Senate are the Appropriations and Budget and Fiscal Review committees. The Budget and Fiscal Review Committee handles the budget. The Appropriations Committee hears any other bills with direct or implied state cost. Thus it can kill almost any major bill.

The Assembly

The Assembly has a form of government that might be called self-inflicted dictatorship. The speaker is elected by at least 41 votes (a simple majority) and thereafter wields tremendous power; this officer appoints all committee chairs and names all committee members except for the Rules Committee. Control over committees amounts to the power to kill any bill. A bill defeated in committee can be brought to the floor by a majority vote of the full assembly, but this occurs very infrequently. A vote to withdraw a bill from committee would be tantamount to a vote of no-confidence for the speaker. The speaker's control over legislation makes whoever holds this office the second-most-powerful official in state government next to the governor. However, on occasion, the speaker has had difficulty leading. Battles within majority Democratic ranks in 1979-80 between then-Speaker Leo McCarthy and challenger Howard Berman, each with his own faction, led to legislative paralysis in the lower house. In 1988 the "Gang of Five" (anti-leadership Democrats) openly feuded with Democratic Speaker Willie Brown over legislative matters in the Assembly. Though the five were punished by Speaker Brown (losing chairmanships, committee assignments, staff and office space) they refused to back down. For a time, the "Five" combined with the Republican caucus had a majority in the Assembly. However after the November 1988 elections, Democrats had 42 seats plus the rebellious "Gang of Five" who were no longer needed for a majority. The "Five" returned to the Democratic fold, and their transgressions forgiven.

The Rules Committee in the Assembly is primarily a housekeeping group, assigning bills to committees, setting salaries for legislative employees, purchasing supplies, and handling routine resolutions.

Speakers come to power in two ways — by the members of the majority party or by coalition. Speaker Willie Brown formed a coalition with members of both parties in 1981.

In the Assembly the key committee is the Ways and Means Committee. It is the general clearing house for most bills before they reach the floor. This is because no measure with fiscal implications — most important bills — can go from a so-called policy committee directly to the floor.

Both houses have become more partisan in recent years. The Senate only a few decades ago paid little attention to party conflict, but the caucuses have become stronger and it is not unusual now to see party-line votes. Partisanship increased in the Assembly during the Reagan, Deukmejian and Wilson governorships. Further fomenting partisanship, party caucuses are active in campaigns for legislative seats, and their staffs are always at work digging up issues that could prove embarrassing to the opposition.

Legislation

There are three basic types of legislation: bills, constitutional amendments and resolutions. These measures can only be introduced by legislators. The governor cannot introduce a bill, but he can ask a friendly member to put it in the hopper. Even the governor's budget carries the name of a lawmaker. In fact, however, very few bills are the direct inspiration of a legislator. Most bills come from interest groups, staff members, constituents, government officials, or a variety of other sources.

A bill is simply a proposed statute. It can be enacted by a simple majority vote in both houses unless it is an urgency measure or carries an appropriation, in which case a two-thirds vote of approval is required. Constitutional amendments are proposed changes to the state Constitution; a two-thirds vote of each house will place one of these measures on the ballot for voter consideration. Resolutions are merely statements of legislative viewpoint. They may be addressed to other governmental agencies, describe state general policy, or commend or memorialize someone. They are normally passed by voice vote. Constitutional amendments and resolutions, unlike bills, are not subject to gubernatorial veto.

Legislative process

When a member introduces a bill, its title is read and it is printed. Then it is assigned to a committee by the Assembly or Senate Rules Committee. The committee hearing is the most crucial stage in the legislative process, for it is at this point — not on the floor — that the fate of most legislation is determined. Following public hearing, the committee can kill the measure or send it to another committee (usually the fiscal committee) or to the floor as is or with recommended amendments. When it reaches the floor, the bill's title is read a second time, amendments are often made, and the legislation is placed on the agenda for debate. After debate, a roll call is taken. If the bill is passed, it is sent to the other house, where the same process takes place. If the bill is amended in the second house, it must return to the house of origin for acceptance or rejection of the amendments. If approved at this point, the bill goes to the governor for signature or veto. If the amendments are rejected, a conference committee of three members of each house is formed to compromise differences. This procedure is always followed on the budget and often used at the end of a session to speed the last-minute rush of bills (because a conference committee report can be produced more rapidly than a revised printed version of a bill).

A bill goes to the governor if both houses approve a conference committee recommendation.

In the Senate, roll calls are taken orally by the secretary of the Senate and aides. Once a roll call is concluded, members may not change their votes, and absent members cannot add their votes. The Assembly uses an electronic vote counter. Members push switches, and lights shine on a board — green reflecting aye; red, no. With the unanimous consent of the membership, members are allowed to change their votes the same day or add their votes if their actions do not alter the outcome.

Legislative modernization

Until 1966, the Legislature met for general sessions in odd-numbered years and for short budget sessions in even-numbered years. Legislators then received $6,000 a year, and their elective positions were not considered to be full-time occupations. In 1966, the voters approved Proposition 1a making each year's session unlimited, raising the pay to $16,000 and allowing lawmakers to give themselves cost-of-living increases of five percent a year. In the June 1990 primary election voters approved Prop. 112. While some of the provisions of this constitutional amendment established new ethics regulations, perhaps its key feature was the creation of a new Citizens' Compensation Commission. The reason this amendment was proposed was because the Legislature angered many votes when they voted to increase their salaries. To deflect this criticism the commission was established. In December 1991 the new commission raised salaries of state legislators from $40,816 a year to $52,500. In

addition, legislative leaders received extra compensation: floor leaders, $57,750 each; and the Speaker and Senate President Pro Tem, each receive $63,000.

In 1972, the people approved another constitutional amendment. This one put the Legislature on the same two-year schedule as Congress, with bills remaining alive for two years. The Legislature now is in session year-round, with breaks for Easter, Christmas, part of the summer and during statewide elections. In addition to their salaries, legislators receive $100 a day for expenses and have use of leased automobiles, credit cards and district offices.

In addition to the standing committees, which consider the merits of bills, the Legislature also establishes two-house joint committees and one-house select committees to study specific problems (often of special concern to only one legislator, who becomes chairman of the committee). These committees can submit recommendations to the Legislature but have no direct power over legislation. Many of these select committees have been eliminated under the new budget strictures of Proposition 140.

Legislative staff

Each member of the Legislature has a personal staff plus the assistance of specialists assigned to committees and to the party caucuses. There are also three major independent bureaus with significant influence on the legislative process— the legislative counsel, the legislative analyst, and the auditor general, although the survival of the two latter offices is threatened by budget reductions mandated by Proposition 140.

• *Legislative counsel*, Bion Gregory, has a large staff of attorneys to provide legal advice to lawmakers and draft their bills and proposed amendments.

• *Legislative analyst*, Elizabeth Hill, provides advice to the Legislature on anything with a fiscal implication, which can cover virtually every major bill. The analyst annually publishes a detailed analysis of the governor's budget, which becomes the basis for legislative hearings on the fiscal program.

• *Auditor general*, Kurt R. Sjoberg (acting), conducts investigations of state agencies to determine whether they can be run more economically and efficiently, he reports directly to the Joint Audit Committee and to the Legislature as a whole.

In all, a staff of some 2,000 served the Legislature until the passage of Prop. 140 in November 1990 which mandated term limits for members and budget reductions for the Legislature. The Legislature's staff has been reduced to comply with the measure. In addition to the analyst, auditor general, and counsel, there are sergeants-at-arms, secretaries, political aides, and committee consultants. The consultants are the most important element of the staff; they provide specialized knowledge for committees, gather information and provide independent evaluation of information obtained from interest groups, the governor and others.

Reapportionment

Almost nothing stirs the juices of a legislator — either at the state or federal level — as much as the prospect of his or her district being reapportioned. Whether as a result of court order or the federal census, redistricting has the potential of throwing many legislators out of office. The census is conducted every 10 years at the beginning of a new decade, and every congressional, Senate and Assembly district in California must be redrawn after each census to eliminate population differences.

California's Assembly districts have always been apportioned by population, but the state Senate has been apportioned under two systems. Prior to 1926, the Senate was also apportioned by population, but in that year the voters approved a "federal plan" devised by Northern Californians to keep control of the Senate from rapidly growing Southern California. This plan provided that no county could have more than one senator and that one senator could represent no more than three counties. As a result, the senator from Los Angeles at one time represented 440 times more people than the senator from Alpine, Inyo and Mono counties. This was the most severe apportionment imbalance in the nation. Such discrepancies were eradicated in 1966, when the U.S. Supreme Court's "one-man, one-vote" edict went into effect.

Redistricting is usually fairly simple if both houses of a legislature and the governor are of the same political party. The party in power merely divides the state to suit itself and gives the opposition party the scraps. The usual procedure is to offer some members of the opposition good deals so that a nominally bipartisan reapportionment bill can be passed. Actually, it is impossible to create good districts for one party without fashioning some just as good for the other. But the legislators doing the redistricting can usually pick and choose whom to favor among members of the opposition. In the 1980s reapportionment, although Democrat Jerry Brown was governor and Democrats had solid majorities in both houses, Republicans stymied the majority party's reapportionment plans by qualifying three separate referenda for the June 1982 ballot. Voters voted "no" against the three Democratic sponsored bills and forced the Democrats to make some adjustments to the district lines.

Under the state Constitution, the Legislature is empowered to reapportion all seats (52 in Congress, 40 Senate and 80 Assembly districts), subject only to a gubernatorial veto. Thus, when a governor is of a different party than the Legislature's leadership an impasse is apt to develop. In this case, either a bi-partisan plan is drawn favoring the incumbents of both parties, maintaining the status quo, or the matter ends up in the courts.

Republicans tried repeatedly in the 1980s to modify the reapportioning process. Their objective was to shift the decision making away from Democratic legislative leaders:

1) In 1982 Republicans joined with Common Cause and qualified Prop. 14 to establish an independent districting commission to do the reapportioning. Voters defeated the proposal.

2) In 1983 then Assemblyman Don Sebastiani qualified a new initiative which provided, he claimed, "fairer" districts than the one the Democrats had devised. This initiative was declared unconstitutional by the state Supreme Court prior to its being voted upon. The court ruled that reapportioning could take place only once each decade.

3) In 1984 Governor Deukmejian authored an initiative to have reapportioning handled by a panel of retired appellate judges. Voters rejected this proposal.

The 1991 reapportionment plans passed by the Democratic-controlled Legislature were vetoed by Republican Governor Pete Wilson. Because of the impasse, districts were drawn by the state Supreme Court with the help of "special masters." Surprisingly, Democrats fared well in 1992 in Assembly, Senate and congressional elections— even with the court-designed districts. 🏛

CALIFORNIA'S LEGISLATIVE PROCESS

INITIAL STEPS BY AUTHOR

IDEA

Sources of bills: legislators, legislative committees, governor, state and local governmental agencies, business firms, lobbyists, citizens.

DRAFTING

Formal copy of bill and "layman's digest" prepared by Legislative Counsel.

INTRODUCTION

Bill submitted by senator or Assembly member. Numbered and read first time. Referred to policy committee by Assembly or Senate Rules Committee. Printed.

ACTION IN HOUSE OF ORIGIN

COMMITTEE

Testimony taken from author, proponents and opponents. Typical actions: Do pass; amend and do pass; no action; hold in committee (kill); amend and re-refer to same committee; refer to another committee; send to interim study.

Bills with any fiscal implications, if approved by policy committee, are referred to Appropriations Committee in the Senate and to Ways and Means Committee in the Assembly.

SECOND READING

Bills given do-pass recommendations are read the second time and placed on the daily file (agenda) for debate on a subsequent day.

FLOOR DEBATE AND VOTE

Bills are read the third time and debated. A roll-call vote follows. For ordinary bills, 21 votes are needed in the Senate and 41 in the Assembly. For urgency bills and most appropriations measures, 27 and 54 votes are required. If these numbers are not reached, the bill is defeated. Any member may seek reconsideration and a second vote. If passed or passed with amendments, the bill is sent to the second house.

ACTION IN SECOND HOUSE

READING

Bill is read the first time and referred to committee by the Assembly or Senate Rules Committee.

COMMITTEE

Procedures and possible actions are nearly identical to those in the first house.

SECOND READING

If cleared by committee, the bill is read a second time and placed on the daily file (agenda) for debate and vote.

FLOOR DEBATE AND VOTE

The procedure is identical to the first house. If a bill is passed without having been amended in the second house, it is sent to the governor's desk. (Resolutions are sent to the secretary of state's office.) If amended in the second house and passed, the measure returns to the house of origin for consideration of amendments.

RESOLUTION OF TWO-HOUSE DIFFERENCES (IF NECESSARY)

CONCURRENCE

The house of origin decides whether to accept the second-house amendments. If the amendments are approved, the bill is sent to the governor. If the amendments are rejected, the bill is placed in the hands of a two-house conference committee composed of three senators and three Assembly members.

CONFERENCE

If the conferees fail to agree, the bill dies. If the conferees present a recommendation for compromise (conference report), both houses vote on the report. If the report is adopted by both, the bill goes to the governor. If either house rejects the report, a second (and even a third) conference committee may be formed.

THE GOVERNOR

SIGN OR VETO?

Within 12 days after receiving a bill, the governor may sign it into law, allow it to become law without his signature or veto it. Bill is sent to Secretary of State's office and given a chapter number. A vetoed bill returns to the house of origin for possible vote on overriding the veto. It requires a two-thirds majority of both houses to override. Urgency measures may become effective immediately after signing. Others usually take effect the following January 1st.

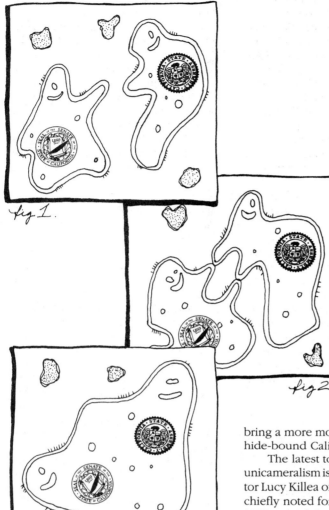

fig 1.

fig 2

fig 3.   PLT

The unicameral legislature

New look at an old idea

By Jim Richardson

Reprinted from *California Journal*, May 1991

A unicameral legislature in California is an idea whose time probably has not come. But amid the ruin that is the California Legislature in the early going of the 1991-1992 session, that age-old idea has surfaced yet again — and not just among the political scientists who find the subject sport, but among the more cynical breed of lawmakers as well.

The outcome of their dialogue likely will not be a one-house Legislature in the foreseeable future, even its more candid proponents admit. But the discussion, some lawmakers believe, could

Jim Richardson is a reporter in The Sacramento Bee *Capitol bureau.*

bring a more modest *perestroika* to the hide-bound California Legislature.

The latest to advance the cause of unicameralism is Democratic state Senator Lucy Killea of San Diego, heretofore chiefly noted for her upset victory in a 1989 special election — an event in part prompted by voter reaction against a Catholic bishop who barred her from receiving communion over her pro-choice views on abortion.

In the spring of 1991, already frustrated in her new job, Killea busily stumped service clubs and lined up political scientists behind unicameralism. Killea proposes establishing a state constitutional revision commission to work out the details. She took a well-publicized trip to Nebraska, the only state with a unicameral legislature. Killea got a fair amount of news coverage on the issue, particularly in her hometown newspapers (where, perhaps not coincidentally, she has been floating the idea of running for mayor later this year).

"We have certainly ended up with gridlock rather than checks-and-balances," said Killea.

But the last thing some of the Legislature's weary leaders want to think

about is a major reform of their institution at a time when they are grappling with a $12 billion budget deficit and have district reapportionment looming just around the corner. Nor have legislative leaders recovered from the legal confusion of Proposition 73's campaign contribution limits, overturned after a long legal wrangle. They are still trying to get used to Proposition 112, a measure they successfully put forward — with varying degrees of enthusiasm — that drastically restricts gifts and bans honoraria for speeches. And legislative leaders are still in deep shock over term limits and accompanying severe budget cutting required by Proposition 140, approved by voters in November 1990.

"The Legislature can only take so much major restructuring," lamented Democratic Senate President pro Tempore David Roberti of Los Angeles, in an interview on Killea's unicameral proposal. "If every time you turn around there is another proposal to restructure the Legislature, quite frankly we'll never get anything done. At some time we have to concentrate on substantive issues."

Killea's argument is that the Legislature has not focused on substantive issues partly because the two houses are so different. Among the contributing factors to the paralyzing budget impasse of 1990, when the Legislature left the state without authority to spend money for nearly a month, was that the two houses could not reach agreement. Each house became consumed in its own politics. At one point, the Senate passed a budget and left town, leaving a fuming Assembly. One Assembly member had choice words for the Senate's action, calling it "dog doo" left on the front porch.

The idea of a unicameral legislature has a certain appeal — doing away with duplicative legislative functions, consolidating dual committees, bringing forth a degree of efficiency and accountability — to lawmaking. Killea maintains that the only thing stopping a unicameral legislature are "artificial reasons" for having two houses and institutional resistance to change.

"I think the sense of crisis around here is causing people to look at it more closely," said Killea. "What we have isn't working. There are a tremendous number of major issues we haven't been able to deal with even in a minor way."

She got a boost to the cause from no less than Republican John Larson on his way out the door as chairman of the state Fair Political Practices Commission. "You can hide too many things with the two houses here," he said in a newspaper interview endorsing unicameralism. "One house will give you anything you want, knowing the other is going to throw it right in the river."

Killea is not the first to push the unicameral idea. Between 1913 and 1937 there were no fewer than 15 proposed constitutional amendments on the subject put forward by California legislators. The idea was revived in the 1970s by the most successful legislator of the modern era — the late Assembly Speaker Jesse Unruh. But 11 such proposed amendments got nowhere.

"The present two-house system is a costly and inefficient anachronism that thwarts the popular will, caters to private interests and hobbles responsible and responsive decision-making," Unruh said in a widely quoted speech. "Unless unicameralism is made central to the present efforts to reform and modernize state legislatures, I do not believe that increased salaries, new facilities, and professional staff will be more than temporary pal-liatives for the ills that it is hoped they will cure. These reforms in themselves only make a more efficient horse and buggy. I take little comfort from the fact that legislatures can be the fastest horse and buggy in the jet age."

Picking up the mantle, Democratic Assemblyman Tom Bane of Tarzana, now the powerful chairman of the Assembly Rules Committee, tried pushing a unicameral legislature in 1975. His bill was approved by a committee dominated by rebels to then Speaker Leo McCarthy. But it went no further. "Some of the people voted for it just because they wanted to have fun," Bane recently recalled.

The current majority and minority leaders of the state Senate, Democrat Barry Keene of Benicia and Republican Kenneth Maddy of Fresno also pushed unicameral bills in the 1970s and early '80s. Keene and Maddy have signed on as co-authors to Killea's bill.

"There's no reason to have two houses," said Maddy, adding he sees "no chance" for Killea's bill (a reality making it easier to support).

In advancing her bill, Killea took a different approach than in earlier efforts. She proposes increasing the size of the Legislature — although she has not suggested exactly to what size. In effect, Killea proposes giving legislators smaller districts, an idea attractive to many who are otherwise loath to a single-house legislature.

Smaller districts are harder to gerrymander. The cost of getting elected theoretically would be less and serving a smaller number of constituents would be easier. Also, the argument goes, with so many more representatives in the Legislature, it would be harder for a narrow special interest to buy or influence enough votes to dominate an issue.

"There is some logic to that," said Senator William Leonard of Red-lands, the second ranking Republican. Although he calls unicameral-ism a "stupid idea," Leonard likes the idea of a bigger Legislature with smaller districts. However, he points out, smaller districts could be achieved without a single-house legislature. Leonard suggested increasing the size of the Assembly by a three- or four-to-one ratio with the Senate instead of the current two-to-one ratio.

Leonard said that despite predictions to the contrary, the Assembly and Senate have each maintained a distinctive character even after court decisions put Senate districts on the same one-person, one-vote basis as Assembly districts. "Here, theoretically, we should all be duplicates of each other. We're not. And I think that's healthy. That means each of us is looking through different eyes at these same bills to see if they read the same way to each of us."

Maddy, however, said that in reality, the Legislature has killed few bills. Roughly 5000 bills per session landed on then-Governor George Deukmejian's desk and there is no sign the number will be appreciably smaller for Governor Pete Wilson. "There is really not a 'check-and-balance' between the two houses," said Maddy. "The trial lawyers are just as strong over there as they are here. They're not checked-and-balanced."

Lawmakers maintain publicly that they have an open mind toward Killea's proposal. However, many say privately — and a few will say publicly — that the real value to her proposal is in spurring a discussion of the Legislature's unwieldy rules.

Roberti and many Democrats have long argued that the single largest impediment to lawmaking is not the dual-house system but the rule that the state budget must be approved by a two-thirds vote in each house. The rule has allowed a small minority of Republicans — sometimes only in one house — to thwart the will of the majority.

The two-thirds vote rule, however, has been next to godliness and the line-item veto in sanctity with Republicans, who have been in the minority in both houses of the Legislature for 20 years. However, some Republicans have begun to change their minds, partly spurred by the discussion over the unicameral proposal. The two-thirds vote has fostered a mentality of being a permanent minority, and in their view, allowed Democrats to escape responsibility for their actions.

"I think we lose in the public relations image every year," said Leonard. "We say we are holding out for something to fill in the blank. The public doesn't buy it. I'm almost of the opinion of saying, 'Look-it, you Democrats, there's a $12 billion problem — you want to run it? Here, you put it out by majority vote. Don't count on me to vote aye."

Then, Leonard suggests, Republicans will be in better position to run for office and become the majority party. "Do you like this? If not, vote for me."

And that suits Roberti fine. "Right now everybody can legitimately confuse the issue as where responsibility lies," said the Senate's top leader. 🏛

Richter

Bronshvag

Brown

Bowler

Rainey

Caldera

Martinez

Escutia

Bowen

Aguiar

Baca

Weggeland

Haynes

Cla

The Propos

By Charles M. Price

Charles Price is a professor of political science at Chico State University and a frequent contributor to California Journal.

Before it ever arrived in Sacramento, the Assembly's "Class of '92" had earned a mark of distinction: It was the largest gaggle of rookie lawmakers to descend on the Capitol *en masse* since 1966 — 26, to be exact (with a 27th about to arrive thanks to a special election in Fresno).

In a typical election, about five or six new members filter out of the Assembly's 80 districts. And with barely a squad of newcomers on the scene, assimilating these few into the Assembly's archane rituals posed only minor problems for leadership. But 1992 was not exactly typical. For a variety of reasons — including anti-incumbent fever among voters, new Supreme Court-reapportioned districts, term-limits-inspired retirements and public anger over legislative scandals and deadlock — about one-third of the Assembly ended up fresh to the ways of politics, Sacramento-style.

The last time Sacramento saw anything like the Class of '92 was 26 years ago, when the 33-strong Class of '66 first wandered through Capitol halls. That election, too, came on the heels of a political revolution of sorts — a 1964 U.S. Supreme Court decision, *Reynolds v. Sims*, requiring both upper and lower houses of American state legislatures to be apportioned on the basis of population. That class was heavy with future political stars; among them Governor Pete Wilson, Secretary of State March Fong Eu, Senate President pro Tem David Roberti, Ways and Means

Snyder

Honeycutt

Knight

Takasugi

Hoge

Karnette

McDonald

Solis

Napolitano

Morrow

Goldsmith

Connolly

Bornstein

'92

140 Babies

Reprinted from *California Journal*, April 1993

chairman John Vasconcellos, former Los Angeles supervisor and term-limit guru Pete Schabarum and newly elected Los Angeles Supervisor Yvonne Brathwaite Burke.

Perhaps some members of the Class of '92 will reach the top of the political ladder, but they will have to climb using fewer rungs. For the Class of '92 is the first group of freshmen and freshwomen to be elected under Proposition 140 — the term limits initiative passed in 1990. Under that initiative, Assembly members may serve a maximum of three terms, or six years. Thus, beginning in 1996, when term limits kick in for those elected to the Assembly two years ago, some 25 to 35 new members will be elected every two years.

The Class of '92 is not unique; it's a harbinger of the future.

In some ways, the neophyte 26 are much like their veteran colleagues: Many have business backgrounds and nearly all have either attended or graduated from college. Besides business backgrounds, there is the usual legislative occupational mix of lawyers, educators and local officials.

However, in a number of other ways the Class of '92 is different than the vets. It reflects what the Assembly will look like in the near future. First, the class is divided almost equally among men and women (14 men and 12 women) and party (14 Democrats and 12 Republicans). Second, about one-fifth of the class is Latino, and for the first time in 12 years an Asian-American (Republican Nao Takasugi) has been elected to the lower house. In addition, Juanita McDonald, an African-American woman, is a member of the class. Significantly, given that any connection to the Legislature was a liability in 1992, only two new members come from legislative staff — a marked departure from the trend of recent elections when many staffers followed their bosses into seats on the floor. In addition, a larger than usual number of the new members had previously held local elective office.

As new Democrat Valerie Brown stated: "Virtually none of the new members came out of state government. They mainly come from local government, local business or community service."

Many of the newcomers are on a sort of temporary leave from family businesses — for example, Kathleen Honeycutt, Bernie Richter and Ted Weggeland. The new crop is, on average, much older than typical first-termers. Republican Assemblyman Weggeland at 29 is the youngest member, but many others are in their 40s, 50s or early 60s. The class includes a number of retirees; among them are ex-law enforcement officers Larry Bowler and Richard Rainey, ex-Air Force officer Pete Knight, former school teacher Betty Karnette, and former Ford claims agent Grace Napolitano. Finally, these appear at first blush to be commuter-legislators. None expressed immediate plans to move families to Sacramento as some career legislators have in the past.

However, the most unique aspect of the Class of '92 is that its members ran for office knowing they would have only a few terms to serve in the Assembly. Unlike Speaker Willie Brown (28 years and counting) or John Vasconcellos (26 years) these newcomers cannot become Assembly careerists. Do these new members consider politics only a temporary interlude? Are they less partisan than senior members? Will they be able to provide leadership to the Assembly in 1996? To help answer these questions, *California Journal*, well, asked the new members.

First of all, none of the newcomers said they were discouraged from running because of the six-year term limit, although a few admitted it was a factor they considered. Indeed, some said they welcomed the short stint. Because of their brief tenure, how-

ever, most newcomers expressed a strong sense of urgency.

"Voters want an end to confrontational grandstanding. They want their legislators to be problem-solvers," said Democrat Betty Karnette, who defeated veteran Republican Assemblyman Gerald Felando in November.

Republican rookie Fred Aguiar added, "This class came with the mandate that we need to get things done."

Indeed, Republican Honeycutt said she and other newcomers were appalled by the tardiness of some of the senior members for floor sessions and committee hearings. "One of the things we [frosh] are doing is coming on time for our meetings. If some of these guys [veterans] were in the business world, they would have been fired long ago for showing up late so often. There is no excuse for this," said Honeycutt.

Republican Ray Haynes argued that since time is short, members of his class are more likely to do what they think is right rather than calculate votes on the basis of getting re-elected. "Whether you serve four years or six years in the Assembly, who cares? Getting re-elected to the same office becomes less important. Term limits changes your focus to concerns about public policy."

When it comes to declaring politics a career, most of the new members consider their stint in the Capitol as temporary. None of the 26 saw politics as a new life, although a pair of Republicans and nine of the Democrats reserved the right to change their minds. Most said they expected to return to their districts after a few terms.

"I don't see myself as a politician because, quite honestly, politics is trying to please all sides," said Valerie Brown. "I'm not that kind of person."

Takagusi, who is in his 70s, said, "At my age, I didn't come up here to be a career politician."

"The people elected under Proposition 140 don't have a pension system or retirement plan," said Democrat Tom Connolly. "So, we must go back to the communities that we come from and live within the rules that we established here."

Connolly felt strongly that new members would have to guard against being swept up by the glamour of the job. "An amazing seduction occurs here," he said. "When was the last time you rode an elevator where the operator knows your name? 'Morning, Assem-

blyman Connolly!' They treat you so well here — better than in my whole life. It would be very easy to start liking this lifestyle too much."

Despite their running under a term-limit system, not all the new members are enamoured of the idea. Republicans seem to like it more, with eight of the 12 supporting the concept, two opposed and two on the cusp. Only four new Democrats support it, however, with seven opposed to term limits and three on the cusp. Nearly all thought that term limits would make members more responsive to their constituents, however.

Said Honeycutt: "I return home each weekend; I shop, go to church, and do business with people who are hurting economically. It was just yesterday that we freshmen were private citizens back in the district." The first termers, she felt, had a more acute sense of the economic problems facing average Californians.

Echoing this sentiment, Democrat Louis Caldera noted: "Much as I appreciate the talent of a lot of senior members, I realize that I've been in the `real world' more recently than they have. And, that's good. But, there are areas of legislative policy that are tremendously complex that can be learned only by experience. There is a real danger that [short-term] legislators will enact the ideas that are in vogue, but not good long-term solutions."

Republican Jan Goldsmith observed, "Right now, we have a good mix between veterans and freshmen, but this won't be the case in the future." Goldsmith worried that the power of the bureaucracy could be enhanced once term limits remove all of the veteran lawmakers.

Nearly all the members (18 of 26) agreed that term limits would have another rippling effect on the state's political system: Members of their class are more likely to challenge incumbent state senators, members of Congress and constitutional officers than were their pre-term-limits predecessors. Only one Democrat thought otherwise, while three Republicans and four Democrats weren't sure.

Thus, these freshmen think the old rule of thumb about not running against incumbents is dead. Of course, plenty of districts will come open, since all state and federal office holders from California now confront limits.

Among the newcomers, Democrats were more opinionated than the Republicans about whether or not members of the Class of '92 would jockey for power early in their careers. Seven Democrats thought it would happen, five disagreed and two wouldn't say. Among Republicans, however, only three thought it would happen, two disagreed — and seven didn't know.

Some of the freshmen thought they had discerned some jockeying within the ranks already. All were keenly aware of one inevitable fact: In all likelihood one of their classmates would be elected speaker in 1996. As Valerie Brown noted: "I'm impressed with the leadership's understanding that we [frosh] are operating within a very different time framework. We need to be prepared to take over leadership by 1996."

Not surprisingly, class distinctions began to emerge between Republicans and Democrats from day one. Democrats received better committee assignments and were assigned more imposing offices than were new Republicans. And for the most part, first-term Republicans were reconciled to these political rules of the game.

One of the most dramatic incidents for the new members came during their orientation when they were informed that because of Proposition 140 budget constraints, each would receive $25,000 less for office expenses than would veterans. The announcement caused considerable consternation and confusion within newcomer ranks, and Republican and Democratic frosh saw things differently.

"One of the things that's going to have to stop is not treating members equally," fumed Republican Bowler. "We all said, 'This isn't right. We all represent the same number of people. To cut our budgets makes us second-class assemblymen and our constituents second-class voters.'"

To quell an incipient rebellion, Assembly Rules Committee Chairman John Burton was called in to talk to the newcomers. According to Bowler, "Burton went into a control mode around the perimeter of the room, bad-eyeing all the Democrats and threatening them."

Subsequently, the new Democrats were called to the speaker's office, and all 14 were later chosen as vice chairs of committees (one new Republican, Richard Rainey, also was selected as a vice chair).

GOP frosh were not amused. As Republican Ray Haynes noted: "The leadership doesn't give a rat's tail about the freshmen. They have lined their pockets at our expense. They have hurt our constituents because they want to maintain their staffs. That's outrageous. The freshmen in the majority party did nothing about it. They were afraid of their own leadership. Of course, they got paid off for doing it. They got the vice chairmanships and extra staff through backfilling, and they stepped on Republican freshmen. We got kicked in the teeth by the majority leadership. Then they say, 'Gee whiz, why don't you like us?'"

In the end, say Republicans, rookie Democrats bailed on them by not attending the newcomer protest meeting.

"We had a real chance there to impact the Assembly and we blew it," said Bowler. "In my heart, I hope that sometime in the future we will be able to work closely with the freshmen Democrats."

From the GOP point of view, although all newcomer budgets were cut, the reductions affected mainly new Republicans because Democratic staffs could be supplemented via their vice chairmanships.

Not surprisingly, Democrats see the incident differently. Valerie Brown said that Speaker Brown's intent in naming the new Democrats as vice chairs was to accelerate the newcomers' learning and get them up to speed as rapidly as possible.

"It was a recognition upon leadership's part that in a few short years [the new members] have to be ready to run the Assembly." In a similar vein, Democrat Vivien Bronshvag noted, "There's been an effort to train and prepare us unlike any previous new class."

"The leadership has been holding our feet to the fire from the beginning," said Democrat Margaret Snyder. "When was the last time you heard of a freshman being selected a vice chair? This was well thought out by leadership."

And, according to Martha Escutia, who heads the Democrats' freshman caucus, Speaker Brown insisted that new Republicans be included in all orientations.

"One of the things I planned for new members was a mock [floor] session — it was great. The speaker encouraged me to include Republicans from the beginning. If he had wanted to be partisan about it, he could have excluded them. After all, knowing the rules of the game helps you to win."

New Democrats were also more sympathetic with the leadership's explanation for the need to cut new members' office budgets. "I could understand the rationale for having first-termers receive less in office budget funds," said Democrat Julie Bornstein. "It was easier to cut us because we hadn't hired our staff." Refuting GOP claims that the vice chairmanships helped provide extra staff, Bornstein said, "None of us have received any extra staff because of our vice chairmanships."

Finally, Democrat Joe Baca argued that it was the Republicans who fired the first partisan shot in the 1993 session. "I thought the speakership election would be the time for everyone to get together and show bipartisan spirit," he said. "The Republicans initially didn't even have a candidate in mind. Their vote for [Minority Leader Jim] Brulte was just a protest vote. That's not cooperation."

Perhaps it is expecting too much to believe that 26 rookies will become something like a new "Gang of 26" and seriously challenge their respective leaderships in the first weeks of the session. After all, they have just barely completed their orientation. They are, first and foremost, Republicans and Democrats, not first-termers.

To their credit, the Assembly frosh have successfully pressured their more senior colleagues into greater punctuality, and this is a good symbolic first step. However, major changes in the way the Assembly operates probably won't come for a year or two, or until the seniors depart.

As Democratic rookie Caldera observed: "Any institution resists change. It's natural. When the seniors are gone, it will be easier to take on some of the sacred cows." 🏛

Update: Indicative of the impact of term limits and the inevitable changing of the guard in the Assembly, three frosh members of the Class of '92 were already made committee chairs by early 1994: Louis Caldera, Banking and Finance; Juanita McDonald, Insurance; and Diane Martinez, Elections, Reapportionment and Constitutional Amendments.

A house soon divided

illustration by Christopher Van Overloop

"Nesting" in the Assembly does not refer to a comfort zone

Reprinted from *California Journal*, July 1993

By A.G. Block

The Senate.

It hangs like mist over the Assembly. It is a half-formed thought, a distant vision not quite in focus yet pulling like magnetic North at the lower house. And its lure among Assembly members may be the unintended consequence of two recent political revolutions — term limits and reapportionment.

Term limits arrived on the wings of Proposition 140, passed by voters in November 1990. Like a lethal plague, it wipes out the careers of every current state senator by 2002. More significant, it drives from office every current member of the Assembly by 1998. Beyond 1998, Assembly members who want to continue in the Legislature must seek the Senate.

In years past, advancement from lower to upper house was blocked by the encrusted nature of incumbency. Senators did not leave until they ran for or were appointed to other jobs, retired or died in harness. As a result, Assembly members often had to wait eons for an opening. Term limits dramatically shorten the wait.

But term limits alone did not create the situation now facing the Assembly, for the 1991 reapportionment also recasts the traditional scramble for the Senate. In the previous redistricting, stitched together by lawmakers themselves, Assembly and Senate districts were drawn independent of one another. Thus, an assemblyman or assemblywoman might represent an area that meandered through several Senate districts, and a vacancy in any one of them might give him or her a shot at the upper house. But in 1991 the process was overseen by the state Supreme Court, and its mapmakers took a more logical approach. They "nested" two adjacent Assembly districts to form one Senate district. Now, an Assembly member who ponders a move to the Senate knows exactly which *other* member is nested in the same territory. Forty potential rivalries were set in stone, and a new internal tension was layered onto the Assembly for the decade of the 1990s.

The chart on page 27 shows the "nestings." In all but seven of the 40 Senate districts, nested Assembly members are from the same party. In most cases, they also are philosophical allies. But alliances and even friendships may prove brittle once members approach 1996 — when a regiment of lawmakers from both houses and both parties are mowed down by term limits.

"You now have two caucuses in the Assembly," said Assembly Minority Leader Jim Brulte. "But the potential exists to have four caucuses. What you have is a structural impediment to caucus unity."

Brulte and others envision an Assembly where members form alliances against other members of their own party, and where some of these unions cross party lines. One member evoked the memory of the Leo McCarthy-Howard Berman speakership fight that nearly paralyzed the Assembly throughout 1979 and 1980, warning that the same bitterness and ferocity generated by that rivalry could revisit the Assembly — only on a grander scale, given the number of members involved.

Hughes   Tucker

Some legislators will be faced with very difficult decisions, a notion expressed by Democratic Assemblywoman Deirdre Alpert of San Diego. Alpert is nested with fellow Democrat Mike Gotch in the 39th Senate District, currently represented by independent Lucy Killea. All three fall victim to term limits in 1996.

"Mike and I will try to work it out ahead of time," Alpert said, adding that it is a knot she has yet to contemplate. She agreed that potential rivalries could further complicate the already complex business of lawmaking. "Just look back at what happened between [Dave] Kelley and [Carol] Bentley last year," she said, referring to the race between two Republican Assembly members thrown together in a vacant Senate district by reapportionment. That contest turned especially bitter toward the end, as did a 1992 Assembly primary involving three Republican incumbents from Orange County — Doris Allen, Nolan Frizzelle and Tom Mays.

"Similar situations have happened in the past," recalled Democratic Assemblyman Richard Katz of Los Angeles. "I remember when [Democratic assemblymen] Dave Elder and Bruce Young shadowed each other over the possibility they would both someday seek Glenn Anderson's congressional seat. It never actually happened, but the notion was there

and it affected how each of them operated."

"It will add an interesting dynamic to the process," mused freshman Assemblyman Ray Haynes, a Murrieta Republican who makes no secret of his desire to challenge Democratic Senator Bob Presley's re-election next year. "You'll see instances of people sniping at each other where you wouldn't expect it."

Haynes, nested with Riverside Republican Ted Weggeland in Presley's 36th District, said he and Weggeland explored the issue before they were elected in 1992. "I saw it as a problem right off the bat," said Haynes. "We reached an accommodation. We're not enemies, even if we run against each other." Weggeland said he's not interested in challenging Presley in 1994; Haynes probably will do it.

Meanwhile, the possibilities for conflict dot California's political landscape. Take the north state's 1st Senate District, where nested Republicans David Knowles of Cameron Park and Bernie Richter of Chico are conservative allies on many issues. The 1st District currently is the province of fellow Republican Tim Leslie of Carnelian Bay. Term limits don't force Leslie out until 2000 — four years after Knowles will be ousted from his Assembly seat and two years after Richter must leave. What do they do? Retire quietly? Or do they challenge Leslie's re-election in 1996? Knowles won't have a choice if he is to remain a legislator. But Richter would still have two years remaining in the Assembly. In years past, it was all but unthinkable for an Assembly member to mount a challenge to a Senate incumbent from his or her own party. But in this era of term limits, all bets may be off. Thus, Leslie, Knowles and Richter — political soulmates all — could be on a collision course in 1996.

Knowles has denied any interest in running for the Senate and said he will be happy to return to the private sector once his Assembly career ends in '96. Knowles admitted, however, that he felt compelled to tell Leslie that he would not challenge him "to preclude any interruption in our relationship." It is significant that Knowles would raise the issue at all — unless he feared Leslie might hear footsteps and thereby threaten their cooperation on matters affecting the district.

The footsteps are real — and loud — in Los Angeles' 25th Senate District. There, Democrat Curtis Tucker Jr., whose Assembly career terminates in 1996, already has informed incumbent Democratic Senator Teresa Hughes that he will challenge her re-election in the June 1996 primary. They may be joined in that primary by Assemblyman Willard Murray, who also falls victim to term limits in 1996. Can Tucker's looming challenge to Hughes do anything but strain their relationship?

Where else will this strain emerge? Democrats John Burton and Jackie Speier are in the 8th Senate District, now represented by independent Quentin Kopp of San Francisco.

Both Burton and Speier leave the Assembly in 1996. Kopp, on the other hand, serves until 1998. If Burton and Speier have any interest in the Senate, they must either challenge Kopp in 1994 or sit idle for two years before running for a vacant 8th District. San Jose Democrats John Vasconcellos and Dom Cortese have terms that end in 1996. That's the same year that term limits end the career of veteran Democrat Al Alquist in the 13th Senate District, where Vasconcellos and Cortese are nested. The Vascon-cellos-Cortese equation is complicated by the fact that in 1992 Vasconcellos did Cortese a favor by taking the tougher of two San Jose Assembly districts in order for the more vulnerable Cortese to have an easier re-election ride.

Most nested Assembly members are from the same party. But in seven Senate districts, they are natural rivals. For example, Republican Andrea Seastrand and Democrat Jack O'Connell share the 18th Senate District. Term limits don't end their Assembly careers until 1996, but the 18th District incumbent — Santa Barbara Democrat Gary Hart — already has announced that he will not seek re-election in 1994. It is said that both Seastrand and O'Connell are seriously considering giving up their final Assembly term to challenge for Hart's seat next year.

presley   haynes

A slightly different situation faces Richard Katz. He and fellow Democrat Barbara Friedman represent parts of the San Fernando Valley. They may serve until 1996, but their Senate district, the 20th, will be vacated by Senate President pro Tempore David Roberti next year — the first victim of Proposition 140. Do Friedman and Katz give up their final Assembly term to seek Roberti's seat? Friedman says she's thinking about it. Katz is still decompressing from his failed campaign for mayor of Los Angeles, but he considers Roberti's seat an option.

Except in a few cases, the "nesting syndrome" hasn't really kicked in around the Capitol. But many members think it will, eventually.

"This will cause a problem," said Republican Assemblyman Paul Woodruff of Forest Falls. "You'll see regional fractionalization and a lot of one-upmanship. You'll see members trying to carve out a political niche" at the expense of another member of their own party. "There are some signs this is happening now," he said, "but out of the spotlight. They gradually will come into the spotlight."

Several members indicated that an ob-vious battle is shaping up inside the GOP caucus between Paul Horcher and Richard Mountjoy, nested in the 29th Senate District now held by Republican Frank Hill. All three are terminal in 1996. Their rivalry is complicated by internal caucus politics, especially Horcher's acceptance of a Ways and Means Committee vice chairmanship that his fellow Republicans agreed should have gone to Stockton Assemblyman Dean Andal. Although the appointment poisoned Horcher's relationship with the entire caucus, observers point out that Mountjoy has been the lead Horcher-basher.

Other allies who may be on collision courses are:
• Liberal Democrats Tom Bates and Barbara Lee in the 9th District, where longtime Democratic Senator Nick Petris leaves in 1996 — the year Bates' and Lee's terms also end.
• Democrats Richard Polanco and Louis Caldera in the 22nd District. Democrat Herschel Rosenthal serves there until 1998, the year Caldera also runs out of time. Polanco, however, is finished in 1996. Does he challenge Rosenthal in 1994?
• Democrats Terry Friedman and Burt Margolin in the 23rd District, where either or both of them could challenge incumbent Democrat Tom Hayden in 1996. Hayden would still have one more term to serve.
• Los Angeles Democrats Gwen Moore and Marguerite Archie-Hudson in the 26th District, where incumbent Democrat Charles Calderon must vacate in 1998.
• Democrats Debra Bowen of Venice and Juanita McDonald of Long Beach in the 28th District. Term limits oust them the same year that 28th District incumbent Diane Watson of Los Angeles must leave.
• East Los Angeles Democrats Martha Escutia and Grace Napolitano in the 30th District, where Democrat Ralph Dills leaves the same year that term limits claim both Escutia and Napolitano.
• Republicans Brulte and Woodruff in the 31st District. They're terminated the same year that incumbent 31st District Republican Bill Leonard leaves office. Woodruff has said he's not interested in the Senate, however.
• Orange County Republicans Doris Allen and Gil Ferguson in the 35th District, where they are forced from office the same year that incumbent GOP Senator Marian Bergeson leaves.

Some observers feel that the tension and rivalries produced by nesting may be good for California, even as it makes life tougher for lawmakers.

"People are going to have to be very careful when they vote on a bill," said one member. "They're going to have to vote in the interest of their districts. They should do this anyway, but a lot of them don't. But with another member ready to stick every vote down your throat, you'll vote with your district."

Minority Leader Brulte thinks there will be another big winner, as well. "The real result of all this," he said, "will be a shift of power to the Senate." Assembly speakers, he argued, might serve only two years and be unable to consolidate power — a situation that could foster bipartisan cooperation in the lower house. "The Assembly will be the minor leagues," he warned. "In the Senate, the pro tem will be there for six years and will become much more powerful than the speaker."

And what will the Assembly be like as the calendar closes in on 1996 and members face political mortality?

"Check the Balkans," said one member. ⛫

LOBBYING & INTEREST GROUPS

The Political Reform Act of 1974 helped reshape relations between lobbyists and legislators. Prior to enactment of this proposition, legislative advocates spent a great deal of time and money entertaining lawmakers and thus winning their favor (and their votes). But the 1974 act prohibited a legislator from taking more than $10 a month from a lobbyist, barred lobbyists from "arranging" for campaign contributions from their clients (this provision has since been invalidated by the courts), established extensive and detailed expense and income reporting requirements, and established the Fair Political Practices Commission to implement the law. The measure has been reasonably successful in cutting the entertainment tie between legislators and advocates and began modifying the way of life in the Capitol. Actually, the system had started to change in 1966 when the Legislature became a full-time body. Many lawmakers and lobbyists brought their families to Sacramento, reducing time available for socializing.

The system today is a far cry from the 1930's and 40's when the late Artie Samish boasted: "To hell with the Governor of California! I'm the Governor of the Legislature." And the state's archetypal lobbyist then was probably right. In his long reign, hardly a bill passed the Legislature without Samish's approval. He raised about $1 million over a six-year period from a nickel-a-barrel levy on beer provided by his biggest client and spent it getting legislators "elected and unelected," as he liked to put it. Until 1953 when he was convicted for income-tax evasion, Samish was dominated Sacramento; other lobbyists were virtually powerless by comparison. Samish's downfall began when he was interviewed for Collier's magazine and posed with a ventriloquist's dummy he called "Mr. Legislature." The resulting embarrassment prodded the Legislature to pass a mild "reform act" technically banning lobbying and regulating "legislative advocates" in Sacramento. But if the activities of lobbyists are not as blatant as in Samish's day, their power continues unabated. Indeed, the increasing costs of running for election — campaigning for a hotly contested Assembly seat can cost more than $1 million — has made lobbyists and the firms that employ them more important than ever. Moreover, the Legislature in recent years has been plagued with a new round of scandals set off by a "sting" operation run by the FBI and the U.S. attorney's office. State Senator, Democrat Joseph Montoya of Whittier, resigned his office after being convicted of taking $3,000 to help secure passage of the FBI's phony legislative proposal, a bill that would have subsidized a shrimp-packing plant on the Sacramento River. State Board of Equalization member Paul Carpenter, a Los Angeles Democrat and former Senator, and two legislative staff members were also been convicted in the "sting." And a third Senator, Alan Robbins, resigned and plead guilty to corruption and is serving time in prison. In the Spring of 1993 Senator Frank Hill and Assemblyman Pat Nolan, both Republicans, lobbyist Clay Jackson and another staff member were indicted as well.

Types of lobbyists

While a few big-name lobbyists who represent stables of clients receive most of the publicity, the corps of advocates includes almost every interest group in the state. In 1993 nearly 900 advocates are registered. They fall into several categories:

• *Contract lobbyists.* These advocates will work for almost any client willing to pay their fee. The most successful of them charge high prices, make substantial campaign contributions and get results.

• *Corporation and trade association lobbyists.* These advocates work for one company and represent only the interests of their firms, although they often work in tandem with other lobbyists trying to reach the same goal.

• *Public agency lobbyists.* Aside from the associations representing public agencies, numerous cities, counties and special districts maintain their own representatives in Sacramento. And most state agencies have "legislative liaisons," though they are not required to register.

• *"Brown-bag" lobbyists.* These advocates represent interests seeking reforms in a variety of so-called public-interest fields. They include numerous organizations with budgets sufficient only for bag lunches.

Lobbying process

Lobbyists operate in several ways. They provide information and arguments on pending legislation in an attempt to win legislators to their point of view. This information function is a legitimate part of the Legislature's work as it helps define issues. Lobbyists also establish friendships with legislators. In addition some lobbyists contribute substantial amounts to campaigns and entertain lavishly on behalf of their clients. Many lobbyists orchestrate appeals from their membership at the local level such as letter-writing campaigns and political participation. Lobbyists also lobby the governor, the bureaucracy, regulatory commissions, the courts and the public.

Lobbyists can succeed because there are a great many bills considered each year about which lawmakers have relatively little knowledge or interest, and a word from a lobbyist may tip the balance. A smart lobbyist knows he or she is wasting time trying to persuade a legislator who has a firm philosophical commitment to one side or another on an issue, and so focuses on the uncommitted lawmaker.

All legislators are susceptible to persuasion by representatives of interest groups. But some are more attuned, for example, to corporate spokesmen, while others are more apt to go along with a representative of an environmental organization. Unlike the Samish days, when the public did not get a clear picture of the happenings in Sacramento, the pleading of teams of the Capitol's most powerful and persuasive advocates now occasionally fall on deaf ears when legislators got a clear message from their constituents. While lobbyists tend to come from within government ranks — i.e., legislators and ex-staff — members retiring from the Legislature because of Proposition 112 of June 1990 must wait one year before going into lobbying. Proposition 112 also prohibits honoraria, limits acceptance of gifts, and restricts compensation for appearing before a state agency. 🏛

illustration by Buz Walker Teach

POWER TO THE TEACHERS

The influential California Teachers Association disproves the old adage: In Capitol politics, those who can, teach.

By Steve Scott

"*T*hose that do teach young babes Do it with gentle means and easy tasks...*"
—William Shakespeare*

The hard-working, selfless teacher, toiling against adversity to bring the light of learning into young minds. It's an ideal firmly embedded in our history and culture — "the Lord's work" in an enlightened society. Thinking about teachers conjures images of Socrates, unlocking the mysteries of thought and logic merely by posing questions to his hero-worshiping students. Or Annie Sullivan, unlocking the very consciouness of Helen Keller with gentle patience and tough love. RobinWilliams in "Dead Poet's Society"; Sidney Poitier in "To Sir With Love"; Robert Donat (or Peter O'Toole) in

Steve Scott is a radio commentator and editor of State Capitols Report.

"Goodbye, Mr. Chips."

With icons like these, one would think teachers have more than a leg up in the public-relations department. So what were the descendants of all those shining lights doing at a San Diego resort last summer, sitting in workshops on grass-roots organizing and voter contact at something called the "Political Action Institute?" They were learning about what, for many teachers, has become as essential as an education degree — political activism.

Sponsoring the institute was an organization that has become, arguably, the most politically influential labor union in the state — the 240,000-member California Teachers Association. Over the past eight years, CTA has doled out more than $3 million in legislative campaign contributions and spent more than $10 million to support or oppose various initiatives. Moreover, CTA has built an unparalleled organizational machine, capable of mobilizing its members on short notice for everything from strike support to political rallies.

Supporters of the CTA say the union is using its clout to wage a valiant struggle to preserve adequate funding for schools. Democratic Assemblywoman Delaine Eastin of Union City, who chairs the Assembly Education Committee, says that "when they're lobbying for or against education issues, it's not just 'what's good for our union?' It's 'what's good for the kids?'"

Critics, however, say the CTA is no different in its exercise of political power than any other special interest group. "There can be some argument made," says Ruth Holton, executive director of California Common Cause, "that because of [CTA's] clout in the Legislature, it is harder for other groups that are just as deserving to get their message heard."

Complaints about the political sway held by the teachers' unions are nothing new; they've been uttered ever since the California Teachers Association formed in 1865. For most of its 128-year history, CTA had a fairly loose admission policy, and a number of administrators were counted among its membership. In the early 1970s the administrators were kicked out, and the organization became involved in the fight over collective bargaining.

At the time, most of CTA's energies were spent competing for members with its arch-rival — the 75,000-member California Federation of Teachers.

But in 1978 the battle for bargaining rights quickly took a back seat to a more immediate, common threat — passage of the property tax-slashing Proposition 13. Although it had formed a political action committee, CTA's scattered and disorganized operation was no match for the initiative's juggernaut, according to Ed Foglia, who in 1978 was beginning the first of two terms as CTA president.

"We came to understand," says Foglia, "that politics is not just a publicity campaign. Politics is door-to-door — the kinds of things that you have to do in order to win elections."

Foglia says he helped develop a "Blueprint for Political Action," — a centralized system of data retrieval, voter registration, absentee canvassing and extensive member education. The political organization tightened and a statewide lobbying and campaign infrastructure began to take shape. That process was hastened in 1983 with the arrival of Alice Huffman as director of government relations. Huffman, an ally of Assembly Speaker Willie Brown, says she "politicized" the organization, helping it to better use its power to influence policy. "I had to teach them that they could do the right thing *and* be successful," says Huffman.

With it's campaign apparatus firmly in place, and a $5 per year assessment on each member's dues for political action, CTA began creeping up the list of heavyweight donors to legislative races, from fifth place in 1985-86 to fourth in 1987-88. In 1989-90 the California Teachers Association's PAC was the Number One legislative campaign donor, giving more than $1 million. In 1991-92 it was in a virtual tie for second with the California Correctional Peace Officers Association, giving just under $900,000.

While contributions at this level automatically make CTA a player, most inside and outside the union mark the turning point in its power and influence to 1988 and the campaign for Proposition 98. The initiative, which guaranteed that schools receive at least 40 percent of the state's general fund budget, was a pent-up response to the erosion in school funding that started with Proposition 13 and continued through George Deukmejian's tenure as governor (1983-90). CTA spent millions to qualify and campaign for Proposition 98, and benefited from the support of state schools chief Bill Honig,

then one of the state's more popular political figures.

When Proposition 98 eked out its narrow victory, schools — and the CTA — found themselves in a unique position. After a decade fighting for funds with the rest of the budget "have-nots," schools were now seen as the biggest "haves" of them all. Almost immediately, they were in court, battling a coalition of children's advocates over whether on-campus health, nutrition, welfare and immunization services would be counted under the 40 percent guarantee.

"Before 98 passed, they went out and asked child-development groups to join them," says Steve Barrow with the Children's Advocacy Institute. "After 98 passed, they sued to remove the child-development programs from underneath Prop 98 protections, putting about $300 million of programs for the most high-risk kids at risk." Ultimately, the state Supreme Court ruled against CTA, and added the programs to the guarantee.

If CTA's relationship with other public advocacy groups is occasionally cool, its relationship with the state's Republican governor is openly hostile. Responding to the pressures of back-to-back budget chasms, Governor Pete Wilson proposed suspending Proposition 98. He also proposed that the age for kindergarten entry be delayed six months. CTA responded with an unprecedented, million-dollar, off-year ad campaign. "We felt it was better to let the public speak, rather than us," said Huffman. "If you have the public joining in, to us it offered more leverage."

The spot, which featured a tearful child being turned away from kindergarten, was heavy-handed but effective, and Wilson backed off the proposal, even though he insisted it was similar to a union-backed plan of a few years ago. The practical effect of the flap was that CTA became "Public Enemy Number One" within the Wilson administration.

"They told a big lie to tell a second big lie, to try to convince people that we had cut school funding," said Maureen DiMarco, Wilson's secretary of Child Development and Education.

CTA officials maintain their actions before and since the passage of Proposition 98 are motivated by a simple and basic instinct — survival. "It's politically popular in this state, right now, to put us in competition with welfare,"

CTA'S SACRAMENTO GATEKEEPER

Well connected and tenacious, Alice Huffman helps keep teachers in lawmaker's faces

One could almost hear the smile on Del Weber's face through the telephone line as a reporter wrapped up a lengthy interview. "When," wondered the California Teachers Association's Republican president, "are you going to ask me about Alice Huffman?"

It is impossible to talk about the rise in prominence of the CTA without also, in the same breath, mentioning Huffman — the union's 56-year-old political director. Based in Sacramento, Huffman directs all aspects of CTA's political strategy, from educating and organizing local members to coordinating statewide initiative efforts.

"She is *the* major force behind CTA's political clout," says Common Cause's Ruth Holton. "She is a very important behind-the-scenes political figure here in California."

Huffman says she didn't seek a career in politics, but rather "politics came to me." A high school dropout, she went to work in 1966 on the campaign of Michigan Congressman Carl Stokes. Urged to move to California "to get a free education," Huffman says she was accepted at UC Berkeley and graduated in two years. She eventually ended up working for Jerry Brown as a deputy in the Parks and Recreation Department.

In 1980 Huffman was invited to join a group being formed by the new Assembly speaker, Willie Brown. The organization was the Black American Political Association of California. "BAPAC caught my fancy more than most of the Blacks working in [Jerry] Brown's administration at the time," says Huffman. "It just seemed to have such promise."

Huffman's ties with Speaker Brown through BAPAC gave her the connections she needed to land a job as a lobbyist with the CTA in 1983. Within a year, she was running the government relations division, and not long after that, CTA's political action committee began showing up among the top campaign donors in the state.

Eventually, Huffman stopped lobbying and began focusing entirely on the political organization. She helped mobilize the coalition that passed Proposition 98 and directed the very successful off-year media campaign last year against Governor Pete Wilson's budget proposals. She also built a "continuing education" program in politics for rank-and-file teachers.

As a tough, no-nonsense operative, Huffman has few peers in Sacramento. "If you're thin-skinned, you don't belong in this business," she says. "There's no way you can work in politics and not acquire enemies." However, her skill and tenacity have also won her fierce loyalty among her CTA colleagues. "She was my only ally at one time on Proposition 98," recalls former CTA President Ed Foglia. "I have a lot of respect for her."

"She's a jewel," gushes Weber.

Perhaps Huffman's closest political association — and her most controversial — is with Willie Brown. Critics of the union charge that Huffman is a conduit through which the speaker distributes campaign money to Democrats.

"[CTA] is a partisan arm of Willie Brown, and that's because of the connection between Willie and Alice," says Maureen DiMarco, Wilson's secretary of Child Development and Education and herself a Democrat.

Lately, these criticisms have been fueled by Huffman's personal crusade to push Brown as a candidate for governor. The effort, which involves gathering petition signatures on Brown's behalf, became immediate fodder for political reporters, and the reaction caught both Huffman and her superiors by surprise.

"All of us were caught up short by the realization that, in today's CTA, you don't have a private life," says Weber, who maintains the Brown campaign has no connection — official or unofficial — with the union.

Huffman insists her campaign for Brown has both a substantive and symbolic value. "No African-American name ever floats for constitutional office," she says. "Willie Brown is the most qualified of all the names floating around. Why not give him a chance?"

As for the broader criticisms of her alliance with Brown, Huffman dismisses them as sour grapes. "They [Republican business interests] used to have a monopoly, but now we're at the table, too. And we have something else they don't — a teacher in every legislative district." 🏛

— **Steve Scott**

UPDATE: In late April 1994 Huffman's work on behalf of another Brown — Kathleen — resulted in her being sanctioned by the CTA. Earlier in the year Huffman leaked the executive committee recommendation for Brown's endorsement and later allegedly briefed her on what were to have been surprise questions.

says CTA President Del Weber. "We're not in competition with welfare. All we're saying is, 'Let's at least hold even with where we are now.'"

The union also points out that it is far from alone in the fight to preserve school funding. Other education organizations, including those representing school boards, administrators and classified employees, have joined CTA and CFT in what's been dubbed "The Unusual Coalition."

"The relationship is very professional," says Davis Campbell, executive director of the California School Boards Association. "There's a real committment to try and stay together as much as possible around that single issue [school funding]."

While the perception of unity among education groups is important, it is CTA's political operation that really gets the job done for teachers. In addition to its deep contribution pockets, the union has one of the most sophisticated grass-roots operations going. Union locals can be mobilized on short notice to man phone banks, walk precincts or host news conferences.

"What makes CTA strong is 'people power,'" says Huffman. "Legislators know that, when they go home, it's teachers they'll be talking to."

According to political consultant Steve Hopcraft, "CTA has the top political operation in the state."

Most of the politicians who benefit from this strong operation are Demo-

crats. "The joke in our caucus is that they're a leisure time subsidiary of the Democratic Party," says Glendale Republican Assemblyman Pat Nolan. "If you deviate from their orthodoxy, they have a tremendous amount of money to pour into your district and tell the voters

that you hate children."

The numbers tell the story. Only three Republican Senate candidates running in 1992 got money from CTA. In the 80 Assembly races, only eight GOP candidates received money from CTA. And only one Republican — Assemblywoman Doris Allen — got the union's self-imposed maximum of $15,000. All told, more than 90 percent of all the money CTA gave last year went to Democrats.

CTA officials counter the charge of partisanship by pointing to their president, Del Weber, who is a Republican from Orange County. Weber says Republican candidates for office get a fair hearing, but he admits to a substantial philosophical divergence between the union and the GOP.

"When you look at the platforms of the two parties," says Weber, "the Democrats tend to vote for things which are better for public education, and they tend to get our endorsements. The Republicans tend not to [vote for public education], and so they tend not to get our endorsements." Huffman adds another point of departure: The GOP's distain for unions. "Ninety percent of the Republicans we interview have a problem with collective bargaining," she says.

The above responses from Weber and Huffman point to the central paradox of the CTA, one that shades its relations not just with the Legislature but with the rest of the education community. On one hand, it is an advocacy organization, seen by many in the public to be fighting the good fight for kids in the classroom. On the other, it is a union, with a clearly defined mandate to represent the interests of teachers. Clearly, CTA benefits from its image as a selfless advocate for education, but where does one role end and the other begin?

For CTA and its supporters, there is no conflict — what's good for teachers is good for schools. "They are a special-

interest group, but every group sees its interests as `special,'" says Eastin. "Some of us see that when your special interest is children and education, you're more on the side of the angels."

Mary Bergan, president of the rival California Federation of Teachers,

vehemently rejects the suggestion that a union identity precludes doing well by students. "I think there are people who would like to think so," says Bergan, "but I don't think that's the case."

To its political adversaries, however, CTA is no less narrow in its focus than doctors, lawyers, insurance companies and all the other "black hat" lobbying interests in Sacramento. "Teachers' salaries are important, but not when you don't have immunization; when you don't have health care; when you don't have basic nutrition," says Barrow of the Children's Advocacy Institute. "They're so protective of their tribe that they've lost sight of the impact [their actions] have on kids."

DiMarco, herself a Democrat, puts it more bluntly: "They're a labor organization, and should not be mistaken for an educational organization."

The one area where supporters and opponents agree is that, ultimately, CTA's success as an institution will be measured not by how many legislators it gets elected, but by the contribution it makes to improving the environment in schools.

"CTA is going to have to have an impact on the workplace," observes Foglia. "Teachers will say [to the union], 'If you're so successful in other areas, how about on a day-to-day basis?' CTA is going to have to continue to evolve in that direction, or else they could very well go down the way other unions have." 🏛

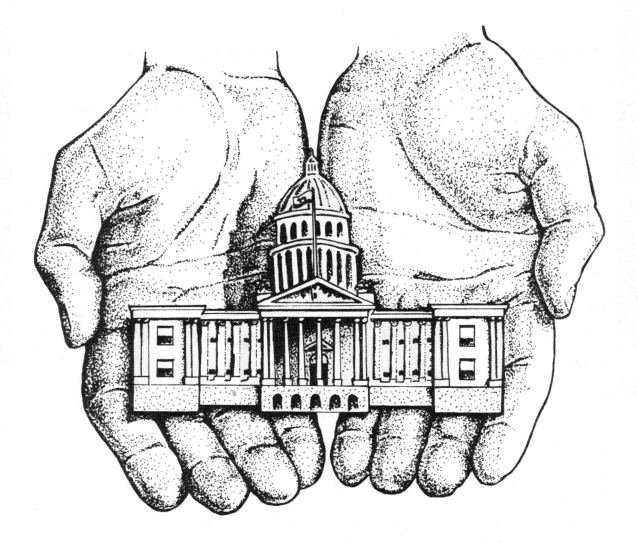

Advocacy in the age of term limits

Lobbying after Proposition 140

Reprinted from *California Journal*, October 1993

By Charles Price

I t never takes much to get a politician talking during an election year, and it seemed the one doing the most talking during 1990 election wasn't even running for office. Pete Schabarum, then a Los Angeles County supervisor, was on the hustings a lot during 1990, hawking Proposition 140, the term limit and legislative budget-cutting initiative. Schabarum would start spinning his term-limit spiel at the drop of the hat, and invariably

Charles Price is a professor of government at California State University, Chico, and a frequent contributor to California Journal.

the topic would turn to "special interests."

"Proposition 140 will remove the grip that vested interests have over the Legislature," thundered Schabarum, to anyone who would listen. "It will put an end to the life-time legislators, who have developed cozy relationships with special interests." Term-limited legislators, it was argued, would be more attuned to the public than they would be to "lobbyists and power brokers" generically identified with most of the evils of politics and government.

Well, the public bit hard on Schabarum's bait, approving both Proposition 140 and the follow-up Proposition 164 in 1992, which limited the terms of California's members of

CAREER LOBBYISTS (6 or more years of experience)		
Classification	**Number**	**%**
multiple contract firms	232	55
corporation	31	7
trade association	31	7
local government	29	6
public interest	26	6
professions/employees	26	6
labor	14	3
farm	11	3
utilities	9	2
health	7	2
miscellaneous	8	2
TOTAL	**424**	**100**

LOBBYING TOTALS: 1975-1994

Year	#Lobbyists	#Employers	$Spent
'75-76	630	795	40,018,666
'77-78	582	760	49,656,908
'79-80	613	857	59,023,150
'81-82	638	1041	58,345,176
'83-84	753	1338	112,519,158
'85-86	838	1695	137,594,247
'87-88	825	1544	158,498,208
'89-90	817	1537	193,578,059
'91-92	886	1455	116,465,129
'93-94	1021	1568	--

Congress. But while most of the focus of the term-limit debate has centered on its effect on career politicians, those "power brokers" continue to quietly ply their trade. Many believe their influence — particularly that of veteran, "career" lobbyists — will increase geometrically when term-limits fully hit their stride in 1996.

Lobbyists have always had a substantial influence in the affairs of California government and politics. Tall tales about the legendary Artie Samish keeping governors cooling their heels in his office abound from those around during the so-called "Golden Days." However, ever since the rules on lobbying tightened following the passage of the 1974 Political Reform Act, lobbyists continued to play a dramatic role in Capitol politics. One reason is sheer numbers.

There are 1021 registered lobbyists in Sacramento — about nine lobbyists for every legislator and more than a third again as many as were around at the time the Reform Act was approved by voters. Just about every group with a product to peddle or an axe to grind has someone on the payroll or on retainer in Sacramento to lobby their interests with the Legislature and the administration. Roughly 41 percent of these lobbyists are what could be classified career lobbyists — six or more years of experience. Veteran lobbyists tend to be white, male and middle-aged — few are African-American or Latino, only about 20 percent are women.

The lobbyists that enjoy the greatest success tend to be those who have been around awhile. "A lobbyist's experience is an important dimension in lobbying," notes Dugald Gillies, a lobbyist in Sacramento since 1967. "Lobbyists who have a public policy memory can be invaluable."

Lobbyists often develop close personal relationships with legislators, relationships that help them gain access and trust. "There are no great lobbyists," veteran lobbyist Judge James D. Garibaldi said shortly before his recent death. "There are only lobbyists with great friends across the street [at the Capitol]."

Until now, the experience of lobbyists has been offset more or less by the experience of legislators themselves. Roughly 11 percent of the lobbyists currently working in Sacramento have 18 or more years' experience in advocacy. By contrast, 16 percent of legislators — 19 out of 120 — have been around that long. Until his death, Garibaldi was the dean of the Third House, having started his lobbying career in 1946. But that still put him behind the dean of the Legislature — Democratic Senator Ralph Dills of Los Angeles, who began his Assembly career in 1938.

As Proposition 140's limits begin to take effect, however, this dynamic will change. Assembly members will be limited to six years in office, with senators limited to a maximum of eight years. This means that the longest any legislator will be able to serve is 14 years — less time than that 11 percent of lobbyists that have been around since 1975. Currently, 41 percent of all lobbyists have been around for at least six years (see chart above). By 1997, if current trends continue, as much as half the lobbying corps will have spent more time in Sacramento than *any* member of the state Assembly — a situation that could be exacerbated when all of those term-limited ex-lawmakers begin lobbying after sitting on the sidelines for the one year mandated by law.

In this kind of environment, the veteran advocate, and his or her client, has a clear advantage. "It takes a couple of terms to learn something about the process," said Garibaldi. "I've got a store of knowledge on wholesale liquor issues that goes back 37 years." Patricia Hewitt, who became one of the first women to work as a contract lobbyist in 1971, agrees. "Experience is critical to lobbying," says Hewitt. "After you get known as knowledgeable in a policy area, legislators and staff will call to get your input on pending legislation."

Since experience is a valuable commodity in any profession, the most veteran lobbyists tend to represent major economic interests and large mass membership groups — the entities with the wherewithal to afford the best. Much of this activity centers around large, multiple-contract lobbying firms — more than half the career lobbyists either run or work for multiple contract firms (see chart, page 30). Most of these firms have one or two lobbyists, representing five to 10 clients. But some of the Capitol's "Jurassic Park" of lobbying have grown to Rexian size. George Steffes employs eight lobbyists and serves 64 clients. Advocation, California Advocates and Sacramento Advocates all employ between three and six lobbyists and carry from 37 to 46 clients. Some of the biggest of the big-shot clients use more than one lobbying firm. Browning-Ferris Industries is represented by no fewer than five lobbying firms. Phillip Morris uses four different firms, and R.J. Reynolds and Whittle Communications each use three firms.

Adding to the strength and continuity of these firms is the people they choose as lobbyists. Some, like Garibaldi and former Senators John Foran and Dennis Carpenter, are ex-legislators. Others include former legislative staff, veterans of prior administrations and governmental agencies, and well-connected lawyers. A large number of career lobbyist firms employ spouses, siblings and sons or daughters, thereby heightening continuity. And then there are trade organizations, which can operate like contract lobbying firms in the manner in which they employ lobbyists. The California Farm Bureau employs nine lobbyists, and seven of the nine are careerists — three of them with more than 18 years experience.

What it all boils down to is knowledge, and in a term-limited Legislature, knowledge translates to power. Without veteran legislators around to "remember when," lobbyists will possess the institutional memory, shaded, no doubt, to reflect the interests of their clients. Moreover, budget cuts imposed by Proposition 140 will mean that legislators will have fewer policy staff experts on the payroll. Lobbyists could wind up becoming surrogate staffers, allowing savvy advocates to not only re-invent the past, but shape the present to their clients' advantage.

"In 1961, the Federal Arsenal at Benicia was slated to be closed," recalls lobbyist Gillies. "I helped put together legislation to allow the city to acquire this property. Now, several legislators have talked to me about using this same principle in their communities with various base closings. Nobody else around here knew about the previous legislation. That's knowledge."

Despite a general sense that experience will help lobbyists gain an edge under term limits, some warn that the experience advantage may be offset by some distinct institutional disadvantages. These disadvantages, argue some, may actually make it tougher for lobbyists familiar with the glad-handing and back-slapping of the "good old days."

For one thing, many of the new arrivals view themselves as "reformers", and thus, tend to be suspicious of lobbyists. "Some of these new legislators won't even talk to you,"

sniffed an exasperated Garibaldi when asked about the 1992 crop. "[They] have a perception that lobbyists are terrible people," adds Hewitt.

Another development that complicates the traditional means of lobbying is the decline of social interaction between lobbyists and legislators. "In the old days, we used to have lunches together and lobbyists, senators and Assembly members got to know each other," recalls Grant Kenyon, long-time lobbyist for the California Restaurant Association. "The rule was that lobbyists would never discuss legislation at these gatherings — just socialize."

Many veteran lobbyists warn that this suspicion and distance could backfire on legislators and, ultimately, make the process less efficient and effective. Many view their experience as a tool that will help make the transition to the post-140 world smoother, if it is used.

"In the business world, people work together over long periods of time," says Kenyon. "That won't be the case with term limits."

Of course, one class of lobbyist will always be welcome — those whose clients also give out campaign contributions. While the terms of office may have changed, the campaign finance rules haven't, and fund-raising becomes even more urgent. "Today, the main interaction between legislators and lobbyists is at fund raisers," says 33-year veteran lobbyist Richard Ratcliff. "I understand from a legislator's standpoint that they have only so much time. They have to raise campaign money, so they have to prioritize who they see based on this."

"This session [the first under term limits] has been business as usual," says 26-year pro Mike Dillon. "My guess is that lobbyists that represent groups with PACs will have a distinct advantage in gaining access."

Still, there are some who see term limits as helping those lobbyists who represent trade, labor and public-interest associations. Leslie Howe, who has lobbied since 1959 and currently represents the California Retailers Association, believes there will be more emphasis on grass-roots lobbying because of the increased turnover occasioned by term-limits. "New legislators are likelier to respond to an interest group's local constituents rather than their Capitol lobbyists," says Howe.

And even if newcomers are suspicious of lobbyists at first, most veteran advocates believe the rookies will eventually seek them out, if for no other reason than simple desperation.

"There's a bill that's been introduced that, if I had known the author, wouldn't have seen the light of day," says Kenyon. "How in the world will people acquire enough knowledge in just four years to be chair of the water committee, for example?"

So what about those "cozy relationships" between special interests and legislators. Will they diminish under Proposition 140? Hardly. Expertise and know-how will continue to reside in the Third House, as will the ever-present pipeline to campaign money. Term-limits mean more turnover, more open seats, and more influence for the lobbyists whose clients can pour money into those seats. And when a lawmaker's time is up, lobbyists can point the way to post-Legislature employment — another of the potential dangers most feared by term-limit opponents. In any case, what the future promises in the Legislature is weak leaders, instability and rapid turnover. What the future holds in the lobbying community is seniority, expertise and influence. 🏛

The fall of Clay Jackson

By Bill Ainsworth

Reprinted from the *California Journal*, January 1994

Once they had decided to convict former lobbyist Clayton Jackson and former Democratic state Senator Paul Carpenter of corruption charges, the 12 jurors in the latest Capitol sting trial still had one more decision to make. Should they also indict a political system that allows special interests to buy votes?

Several jurors argued that they should send a letter to the judge saying that the real villain in the case is a system where money buys power and influence.

"They [the defendants] are victims of our system," said Ali Ardeshir, a juror and engineer. "There is a very thin line between what is illegal and what is legal."

Jurors, who took six days before reaching their verdict, chose not to send their letter, but some of them expressed their feelings in a private meeting with U.S. District Judge Edward Garcia, who presided over the case.

"We told him that if the system wasn't so loose, maybe people wouldn't be getting into such deep water," said juror Nitya Judal, a secretary.

During the six-week trial, jurors got a glimpse of how Capitol powerbrokers operate behind the scenes. They were disgusted by what they saw. The case featured two smug, money-hungry legislators and a boastful, arrogant lobbyist. It also raised disturbing questions about the connections between money and power at the Capitol.

"How can a certain group of people that nobody even voted for run the government?" asked juror Robert Bartosh.

Jurors found Jackson guilty of racketeering, conspiracy and mail fraud for bribing former Democratic state Senator Alan Robbins. They also found the 65-year-old Carpenter guilty of laundering money for Robbins. The prosecutions were part of a seven-year FBI sting investigation into Capitol corruption.

Bill Ainsworth is Sacramento correspondent for the San Francisco Recorder.

Jackson's conviction ended the 23-year career of the state's premier lobbyist, a man once welcomed in insurance corporate board rooms, the governor's office and the halls of the Legislature. No other lobbyist in Sacramento possessed his combination of contacts, control over campaign contributions and knowledge of the important area of insurance. Jackson's firm, SRJ Jackson/Barish & Associates, regularly topped the list of the state's highest-earning lobbying firms. In 1992 he personally earned $300,000 from the firm. In addition, he earned high fees as an insurance lawyer and managing partner for Sullivan, Roche & Johnson, a prestigious San Francisco law firm founded by California Governor Hiram Johnson. In his spare time, the 50-year-old lawyer-lobbyist taught ethics at San Francisco Law School. Though a workaholic, Jackson enjoyed the luxurious lifestyle — including a full-time chauffeur and a yacht — made possible by his high earnings. Now he faces five to 10 years in federal prison. Sentencing is set for February 14.

At the heart of the case against Jackson were tapes that showed him trying to raise $250,000 for Robbins in exchange for help for his insurance clients. Robbins had secretly tape-recorded conversations with Jackson as part of a deal he made with prosecutors in the summer of 1991 to reduce his own five-year sentence for tax evasion and racketeering down to two years. He pled guilty and resigned his seat in the Senate in November 1991.

While working as a government informant, Robbins, the powerful chairman of the Senate Insurance Committee, told Jackson he could do his insurance clients a big favor: move jurisdiction for workers-compensation insurance issues from the Senate Industrial Relations Committee to the "friendly" confines of the Insurance Committee.

On the tapes, Jackson promised Robbins that he would raise $250,000 for the senator in exchange for Robbins' efforts. In subsequent conversations, he repeatedly discussed attempts to come up with the money and even expressed a willingness to launder it. At one point, Jackson tells Robbins that "all I need to do is pull a trigger" to raise $50,000.

In his closing arguments, prosecutor John Vincent, assistant U.S. attorney, said the tapes captured the "the uncut, uncensored Clay Jackson." And Vincent said he was outraged by Jackson's attempts to buy legislative favors. "It's enough to make you throw up," he said.

Jackson's attorney, Donald Heller, countered that Jackson was the victim of an extortion attempt by Robbins, who was trying to trap the lobbyist to shave time off his own prison sentence. Jackson never raised any bribe money; Heller contended that he was merely playing along to placate a money-hungry legislator. Throughout the trial, Heller relentlessly attacked Robbins' motives, reputation and credibility. "In Alan Robbins, you have the coalescence of intelligence, cunning, amorality and evil," he told the jury.

Even the lead FBI investigator for the prosecution, James Wedick, admitted that before Robbins agreed to cooperate, "he was one of the most evasive people I have ever had the opportunity to question." To the jury, "evasive" was a charitable description of Robbins. Some jurors called him a "sleaze" and a "liar." The six jurors interviewed for this story said they took special care not to convict the defendants solely on Robbins' word.

As a result, the jury deadlocked on three acts of the racketeering charge against Jackson in which the main evidence was Robbins' testimony. The acts involved legally reported campaign contributions to Robbins from three separate Jackson clients — convenience store owners, Surety Company of the Pacific and G-Tech, a lottery contractor. In each case, Robbins testified that the contributions were bribes.

In other cases, though, the prosecution produced tapes of Robbins' conversations with Jackson. The jury believed that those tapes proved conclusively that Jackson had attempted to bribe the senator. None of them bought Jackson's story that he was only pretending to appease Robbins because he feared him.

Jackson's contempt for his colleagues, his taped boasts about his power, and even his physical appearance worked against him. On the tapes, he called Insurance Commissioner John Garamendi a "twit," derided his insurance clients as "idiots" and called his ally, Governor Pete Wilson, "somewhat inept." The heavyset, six-foot, six-inch defendant, a former offensive tackle on the football team at the University of Southern California, repeatedly bragged about his power and influence with Wilson.

"The way Jackson carries himself and his behavior showed that he wasn't a person who could be intimidated by anyone," juror Ardeshir said. "He had the power and the money. In his mind, he had the power to buy anyone."

Indeed, Jackson gained his reputation partly by his ability to direct or withhold campaign contributions to legislators. Even before his trial and conviction, he was known for his willingness to use his clients' money to influence legislation. "A lot of his power comes from bringing a money bag to the Capitol," said a veteran lobbyist in a 1991 interview.

On the tapes, Jackson boasted that he had so much control over the campaign contributions of his clients that he could even convince them to donate to state Senator Tom Hayden, a liberal Santa Monica Democrat despised by most business interests. Frequently, Jackson's clients gave out more than $1 million a year in contributions.

Jackson came to the capital in 1970, after graduating from Hastings Law School. He quickly mastered politics and parliamentary procedure and began to develop his specialty in insurance regulation. Starting with the California Hotel and Motel Association, Jackson gradually built up an impressive client list. In a 1991 interview, he conceded that money was part of his success. "Delivering accurate information is a big part of being a good lobbyist," he said. "But so are contacts and support of the political system. Unfortunately, money is a big part of the political system."

Jackson's reputation for success in the Legislature attracted blue-chip clients, including Anheuser-Busch, Proctor & Gamble, B.F. Goodrich and the American Insurance Association — a group of 250 giant insurance companies. Even after he was publicly accused of bribery, but before his indictment, most of Jackson's clients remained with his firm. And Capitol policy makers continued to grant him access.

Just three months before his indictment, former Wilson cabinet secretary Loren Kaye called Jackson a "credible, straight-shooter" welcome inside the governor's office. At the time, Jackson said he was not surprised that doors of powerful policy makers were still open to his firm. "They know us," he said. "They know how our operation works."

Jackson was also popular among his fellow lobbyists. When he was indicted in February, 30 lobbyists signed a letter of support for him. They also pledged $100,000 toward a legal bill that could cost him up to $1 million. Many lobbyists supported Jackson because they feared that his prosecution was an attack on the campaign-contribution system. Some allegations against him involved legal contributions that Robbins claimed were bribes only years later. Lobbyists worried that anyone whose clients gave money to lawmakers could risk similar prosecution.

Jackson's conviction has only confirmed their fears. Many lobbyists are now worried that the U.S. attorney's office has blurred the line between legal contributions — an everyday part of state politics — and illegal bribes. A lawmaker could turn a lobbyist into a criminal by claiming that a contribution was a bribe, they say. "I worry that more people are going to cross the line before they realize it's too late," said one lobbyist.

Several lobbyists said they would move to put more distance between their roles as policy advocates and fund raisers.

"The message is clear. Anybody who is involved in fund raising and policy ought to make sure not to mix the two," said George Steffes, one of the state's most prominent lobbyists.

One veteran lobbyist worried that the public exposure of Jackson's crass tactics would tarnish the reputation of the 1000 lobbyists in Sacramento. He believes the profession of lobbying has been unfairly convicted. "The trial confirmed the public's worst suspicions about lobbying," he said. Even legendary liquor lobbyist Artie Samish, who publicly boasted that he controlled the Legislature the same way a ventriloquist manipulates his dummy, did not do as much damage to the profession. "It did more harm to lobbying than Artie Samish could have ever dreamed of," he said.

Several jurors in the Jackson/Carpenter trial said they would welcome public financing, contribution limits or any changes that would reduce the influence of money over policy. The jurors, exposed to the underside of lobbying and deal-making at the Capitol for six weeks, did not like what they saw. Lobbyists exert too much power on behalf of wealthy clients, they concluded.

"The more I learned about the system, the more I hated it," said Ardeshir. "These lobbyists have so much power because they've got money to throw around left and right." 🏛

PARTIES, POLITICS & ELECTIONS

Political Parties

By both design and tradition, political parties in California are exceptionally weak — especially when compared to the machine politics prevalent in some eastern states. The weakening of the party structure was engineered by Hiram Johnson and the Progressives starting in 1911 as a reaction to the machine politics of the railroad interests and San Francisco boss Abe Ruef. Parties were explicitly forbidden from endorsing in non-partisan contests and implicitly from making pre-primary endorsements in partisan contests for much of this century. All local offices and judgeships were made nonpartisan, and a unique method of running, called cross-filing, was instituted. Numerous provisions were written into the law for the express purpose of reducing party power, and many of these restrictions remain in the law today. An independent spirit was fostered in California, and even now there are parts of the state where the electorate pays very little attention to a candidate's party. It is these areas — notably the San Joaquin Valley and the rural districts that can hold the balance of power in state elections.

Under cross-filing, which lasted from 1914 to 1959, a candidate could file for the nomination of not only his or her own party but other parties as well (and until 1952, without any indication of party affiliation). This had the effect of weakening party structure and making pressure groups and the press more important. It also led to the election of popular candidates in the primary, when they won both the Republican and Democratic nominations. Generally, cross-filing helped Republicans more than Democrats, and it is probably significant that Democrats have done much better in elections since the system was eliminated in favor of traditional primaries.

California now has six official parties — Democratic, Republican, Libertarian, Peace and Freedom, American Independent, and as of 1992, the Green Party. A party can win official status by getting the signatures of one percent of the registered voters or by obtaining a petition signed by a number of voters equal to ten percent of the votes cast for governor in the previous election. To remain official, a party must get two percent of the vote for a statewide candidate and retain one-15th of one percent of registered voters. Loss of official status means that a party can run candidates by write-in only, a difficult assignment in an era of electronic voting.

Party organization

The party structure is spelled out in detail in state law, although some minor variations are allowed for Democrats and Republicans. These are the basic official elements of party structure:

• *National committee members.* These are elected by the delegation to the national convention and serve as the state party's representatives on the national committee of each party.

• *Delegates to national convention.* Slates are developed by supporters of each primary candidate, and winning delegates — with alterations and additions — cast the state's votes at the quadrennial convention. The winner-take-all primary is used by California Republicans. State Democrats use a proportional representation system of delegates elected from congressional districts.

• *County central committees.* These committees, elected directly by the voters, are charged with directing party affairs in each county. In fact, however, these committees are weak, and the real power is held by the office-holders in each county.

• *State central committee.* This committee is comprised of about 1400 members in the GOP and 2500 to 3000 members in the Democratic Party. This committee is charged with electing party officials, managing and operating the party, and selecting presidential electors. An executive committee of the state central committee handles the day-to-day operation of the party.

• *State chairman.* In theory, the chairman speaks for the party and develops election strategy in conjunction with the executive committee. With rare exception, however, the main leaders are the major office holders of both parties.

As noted, Progressive reforms weakened party organization in the state. However, several new developments may serve to strengthen California parties:

1) Because of court rulings in the 1980s, parties may now make endorsements in partisan primaries. (They are still prohibited from endorsing in non-partisan contests.) Democrats have established detailed regulations for their party on their endorsing rules and format. Republicans have decided, because of potential divisions, not to endorse. Since 1988, (the first year that endorsing went into effect), endorsing has not been a major factor influencing the nomination or election politics of the Democratic Party, but it could evolve into a significant factor in the years ahead.

2) Parties have democratized selection to State Central Committees. There are fewer appointments by office-holders, and more elections from the counties. Democrats have created Assembly District Caucuses in the 80 districts to choose 12 delegates per district.

3) Lastly, election by Democrats of Jerry Brown (former governor and ambitious elective office seeker) symbolized the growing importance of the state chair's position. Current state chairs are Bill Press for the Democrats and Tirso del Junco for the Republicans.

POLITICAL PARTY ORGANIZATION

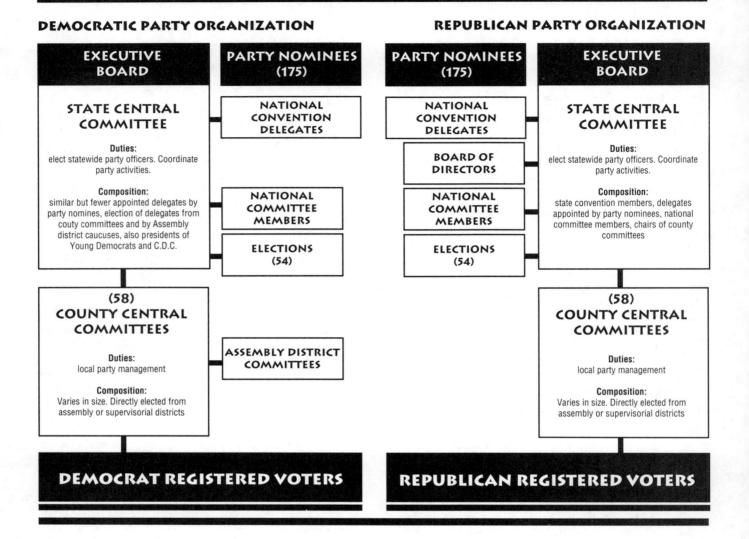

DEMOCRATIC PARTY ORGANIZATION

EXECUTIVE BOARD

STATE CENTRAL COMMITTEE

Duties:
elect statewide party officers. Coordinate party activities.

Composition:
similar but fewer appointed delegates by party nomines, election of delegates from couty committees and by Assembly district caucuses, also presidents of Young Democrats and C.D.C.

PARTY NOMINEES (175)

NATIONAL CONVENTION DELEGATES

NATIONAL COMMITTEE MEMBERS

ELECTIONS (54)

(58) COUNTY CENTRAL COMMITTEES

Duties:
local party management

Composition:
Varies in size. Directly elected from assembly or supervisorial districts

ASSEMBLY DISTRICT COMMITTEES

DEMOCRAT REGISTERED VOTERS

REPUBLICAN PARTY ORGANIZATION

PARTY NOMINEES (175)

NATIONAL CONVENTION DELEGATES

BOARD OF DIRECTORS

NATIONAL COMMITTEE MEMBERS

ELECTIONS (54)

EXECUTIVE BOARD

STATE CENTRAL COMMITTEE

Duties:
elect statewide party officers. Coordinate party activities.

Composition:
state convention members, delegates appointed by party nominees, national committee members, chairs of county committees

(58) COUNTY CENTRAL COMMITTEES

Duties:
local party management

Composition:
Varies in size. Directly elected from assembly or supervisorial districts

REPUBLICAN REGISTERED VOTERS

Elections

A person may register to vote in California who is 18, a citizen of the United States and a resident of the county of registration for at least 30 days prior to the election (and who is otherwise not disqualified, such as in the case of certain felons). There are several types of elections in California:

• *State primaries.* These take place the first Tuesday after the first Monday in June of even-numbered years. At these elections, nominees for national, state and some local offices are selected. Usually, there are a number of propositions also on the ballot.

• *State general elections.* These take place on the first Tuesday after the first Monday in November of even-numbered years, and voters make their selections from among the nominees chosen in the primaries. The ballot usually contains more propositions.

• *Special elections.* These rarely take place on a state-wide basis because of high cost, although there was one in November 1973 when Governor Ronald Reagan put his tax-limitation initiative to a vote (it lost). Special elections are more often held locally to fill vacancies in Congress and the state Legislature. These are different from most other elections in that the voters are given a list of candidates of all parties. If no one candidate receives a simple majority, a runoff is held four weeks later among the top vote-getters in each party. In some cases, this means that candidates far down the list make the runoff while the candidate who finished second in number of votes does not.

• *Local elections.* Often, elections for local city council and special district-director posts are not consolidated with the primary and general elections and are held at various times during the year.

Political History

During the early years of state history, there were rapid political swings based on economics. When things went well, the big-business interests were in control. During a depression period in the 1870s, the Workingmen's Party under Denis Kearney of San Francisco came to power and managed to get much of its program enacted. When prosperity returned, the party disappeared. Economic and political power went into the hands of the "Big Four" — railroad magnates Charles Crocker, Mark Hopkins, Collis P. Huntington and Leland Stanford. Southern Pacific dominated California politics from the 1880s until the advent of the Progressives more than 25 years later.

The Progressives

Republican newspaper editors started in the first decade of this century to drum up opposition to the railroads and the boss of San Francisco, Abe Ruef. Disgruntled Republicans started the Lincoln-Roosevelt league, and graft-fighter Hiram Johnson became the group's candidate for governor. He pledged to kick Southern Pacific out of the Republican Party and out of California government. He won easily and immediately started enacting reforms such as the initiative, referendum, recall, cross-filing, civil service, and a multitude of other programs. Johnson went to the United States Senate in 1916 and was succeeded by another progressive, William D. Stephens. The movement lost its force in the 1920s as postwar prosperity produced political apathy. Until the next depression, the regular Republicans maintained control of state government.

The Great Depression resulted in the 1934 gubernatorial candidacy of muckraking author Upton Sinclair (his slogan: "End Poverty in California") with his radical plan for reforming the economic system. Republican Frank Merriam defeated Sinclair by about a quarter of a million votes. With the Democrats riding high nationally under President Franklin D. Roosevelt, the Republicans finally lost the governorship in 1938 to state Senator Culbert Olson.

Four years later, a new progressive era began under Earl Warren. Aided by cross-filing, the former Alameda County district attorney and state attorney general portrayed himself as a non-partisan official — an image he embroidered later as an activist Chief Justice of the United States. Warren's personal popularity was unprecedented in California political history. He was able to push most of his programs through the Legislature (with a compulsory health-insurance plan the notable exception). Warren was the Republican vice-presidential nominee in 1948 (with Thomas Dewey) and perhaps could have remained governor indefinitely. After 10 years as the state's chief executive, he was named U.S. chief justice by President Eisenhower in 1953.

The new governor was Goodwin J. Knight, who was reelected in his own right in 1954 but was unable to establish himself as leader of the Republican Party because he had to contend with two other major figures, then-Vice-President Richard Nixon and U.S. Senator William Knowland. In 1958, Knowland decided that for political and personal reasons — he thought being governor was a better stepping stone to the presidency — he would leave his safe Senate seat to run for governor. Knight was pushed aside and virtually forced to run for Knowland's seat. Knowland embraced a right-to-work initiative, setting the stage for a massive Democratic victory led by the gubernatorial candidate, Edmund G. (Pat) Brown. Nixon, defeated in a 1960 run for president against John F. Kennedy, tried an unsuccessful comeback by running against Brown in 1962.

In his second term, Brown became embroiled in a bitter intra-party fight with the powerful speaker of the Assembly, Jesse M. Unruh, and elected to seek a third term rather than give his arch-rival a clear shot at his job. In the primary election, Brown's forces concentrated on shooting down the moderate Republican candidate, former San Francisco Mayor George Christopher, preferring to run against the conservative Ronald Reagan, a former actor. Somebody goofed: Reagan crushed Brown in the general by a million votes.

Democratic nominee Unruh tried to unseat Reagan four years later. Although plagued by limited financial resources, Unruh cut Reagan's victory margin in half. Reagan kept his 1966 pledge not to seek a third term in 1974, leaving the gates wide open. Twenty-nine candidates ran in the primary, with Brown's son, Jerry, and Houston I. Flournoy emerging from the pack to represent the Democratic and Republican parties in November. Brown won by only 179,000 votes, almost blowing his big early lead. Four years later, he rebounded with a 1.3-million-vote victory over the GOP attorney general, Evelle J. Younger.

In 1982 Jerry Brown continued the two-term limit tradition and ran for U.S. Senator (he lost to San Diego Mayor Pete Wilson, a Republican). Attorney General George Deukmejian won a tough primary against Lieutenant Governor Mike Curb for the Republican party nomination and squeaked past the Democratic candidate, Los Angeles Mayor Tom Bradley, in November.

In a repeat in 1986, Deukmejian trounced Bradley, winning by over a million and a half votes. Alan Cranston won re-election to a fourth term in the U.S. Senate, defeating Republican Rep. Ed Zschau.

Pete Wilson maintained Republican control of the state's chief executive position with his victory over Democrat Dianne Feinstein in November 1990. Wilson's non-ideological, pragmatic philosophy is more in the Warren, not Reagan, mold.

For the first time this century both U.S. Senate seats were up for election in 1992, the extra seat as a result of Pete Wilson's resignation from the Senate, and for the first time in the nation's history two women, Democrats Dianne Feinstein and Barbara Boxer, were elected the the U.S. Senate. 🏛

Did 1992 herald the dawn of Latino political power?

illustration by Lynwood Montgomery

Reprinted from *California Journal*, January 1993

By Dale Maharidge

One August day in the summer of 1970, 12-year-old Martha Escutia was mowing her grandfather's lawn in East Los Angeles. A few blocks away, cops were tear-gassing 5000 Chicano protesters. Escutia's parents kept close reins on their daughter to keep her away from trouble. Anything could happen, as journalist Ruben Salazar was to learn that day. After covering the riot, he stopped for a beer in a Whittier Avenue bar when it was unexpectedly surrounded by Los Angeles sheriff's deputies. A tear-gas shell blasted point-blank into the bar hit Salazar, killing him. Although Salazar's death was ruled accidental, it smacked of an execution and made him into a martyr. Salazar is no Latino version of Malcolm X, but as a *Los Angeles Times* columnist and *KMEX-TV* news director, he was *the* voice for area Latinos. He pushed hard on stories such as Latinos dying with mysterious regularity while in sheriff's custody.

At that time, Latinos had no real voice in California state politics: None were in the state Senate (the last time a seat was held was in 1913); in the Assembly, there was just one Latino.

The Latino community made political gains over the next two decades, but the 1992 elections heralded the biggest change in this century — a record 10 Latinos in the Legislature. All the action was in the Assembly, where there was an increase from four to seven seats (three more are in the Senate), with six going to freshmen — including the now-

---

Dale Maharidge is a Pulitzer Prize-winning author and former reporter for The Sacramento Bee. *He currently teaches journalism at Stanford.*

grown Martha Escutia.

Escutia and the others are heirs to a legacy with its roots in a Chicano movement that took Latinos from the streets to the halls of power in numbers not seen in modern times. Many are unaware that in 1847, the military governor of California had seven advisers, four of them Latino. And the new state's Legislature from 1849 through 1864 had mostly proportional Latino representation, before the long drought began.

"This is the starting point for the next major shift for Latino power in California," said Richard Martinez, executive director for the Southwest Voter Registration Education Project.

Reapportionment by the state Supreme Court that created heavily Latino districts is certainly a factor but does not entirely account for the change. The Latino community, the largest minority in the state but long considered politically impotent because of low voter turnout, is no longer dormant.

"The sleeping giant is awakened," said 45th District Assemblyman Richard Polanco, a Democratic incumbent who easily won re-election. "The myth of the past is that, a myth."

Polanco's hyperbole notwithstanding, there are indications of increased Latino involvement — that the giant may be awake. At least, its eyelids are fluttering. Whether or not it is ready to sit up and aggressively flex its muscles remains to be seen.

In the past, Latino voter-turnout rates have been low for a variety of reasons, among them: Major parties have viewed Latinos as invisible and thus have spent little time trying to energize them; unfavorable gerrymandering of districts split the Latino community among various neighboring districts to enhance Democratic chances in those districts; a large chunk of the Latino community was ineligible to vote because they weren't citizens or were underage. Yet Latino activists have argued that if the community had a chance to have a meaningful voice, it would get involved.

The 1992 elections seem to offer some glimpse of the future. In 1988, 7.5 percent of the total votes cast statewide for president came from Latinos. In 1992 it jumped to 10 percent, meaning 1.15 million California Latinos went to the polls, according to Mark DiCamillo, associate director of The Field Poll.

"This was the first little tick upwards that we noted," DiCamillo said of the years of stagnant voting patterns. "The registration efforts are finally starting to pay off. And more Latinos are running in Assembly and congressional races, so this has increased participation."

While notable, Latino increases in the Legislature still are relatively low. In the Assembly, for instance, Latinos represent 8 percent of the legislative body, while they make up 25 percent of the California population.

There seems to be an invisible wall at the Tehachapi Mountains; all Latino legislators are from south of that line. That situation could change this year in the race for an Assembly seat being vacated by Democrat Bruce Bronzan. At

> **I** do not see myself as a Latino politician in that this is the only community I represent. You're only going to be relevant if you address issues of all Californians, not just one community.
>
> **— Louis Caldera**

least one strong Latino candidate intends to run in the Central Valley district — Bronzan's district director, Cruz Bustamante. And there are plenty of local Latino officeholders in the north poised to run in future legislative races.

One thing is certain: There certainly is no going back to the old days when the only Latino politician of note was Congressman Ed Roybal. A look at Latino politics is a search into the recent and powerless past. Paging through yellowed copies of *La Raza*, a magazine begun in 1970 as a voice of the Chicano movement, one senses there was a never-ending Los Angeles riot in those years. Dozens of pictures show Latinos being held in headlock or pummeled by law officers.

The bloody street battles, if not directly responsible for political gains, at least raised awareness to make change possible. The first Latino legislators who came into office, however, were held up as oddities, the subject of much scrutiny, not only among the press but among their fellow lawmakers. There also was a focus on Latino infighting that reached legendary proportions during a bitter 1982 state Senate primary between incumbent Democrat Alex Garcia and Assemblyman Art Torres. Torres ousted Garcia, but the contest took its toll.

Lately, that infighting has involved Los Angeles County Supervisor Gloria Molina (a former assemblywoman and the first Latina elected to the Legislature in 1982) vs. "the guys" — usually Polanco, Torres, and Los Angeles Councilman Richard Alatorre, also a former assemblyman. This was not a Latina-Latino confrontation, however, since both sides supported both male and female candidates.

The intrigue reached a peak during June's primary when the two camps supported different candidates in most Assembly races in Latino-dominated districts. Molina's camp was the loser, with its only victor being Hilda Solis of the 57th Assembly District in El Monte. The infighting has been the cause of thousands of hours of gossip, has meant the use of untold gallons of printing ink, and has resulted in anger among Latino leaders — not at each other but at the way the factions have been reported.

"No one says the Anglos are going at each other," said Martinez of the Southwest Voter Project. "The Legislature is lousy with factions: Anglos have factions, African-Americans have factions. We're no different than anybody else."

The battle between camps will not continue, according to Solis, who said: "I will be independent. I owe people in my community. I think it's unfortunate that kind of stuff has gone on."

The increased number of Latino legislators also may mean Latinos have reached political maturity, at least in the eyes of other ethnic groups that no longer will have just a handful of Latinos to talk about. And the freshmen differ from past Latino lawmakers. One clear distinction is that four of the six newcomers in the Assembly are women. While this sudden jump might seem surprising, it is a natural and expected evolution, said Richard Santillan, director of the

Ethnic and Woman's Studies Department at California Polytechnic University in Pomona.

"It's not surprising to any of us who study Latin American politics," Santillan said. "Women have always been involved in political organization, around the church, the school. I can trace this back to the 1920s and the 1930s."

In the past, women remained in the background, supporting male candidates, Santillan said, but they are no longer going to stay there. And he added that while many Latino politicians of the recent past came out of labor unions, the newcomers come out of private industry, legal careers, the non-profit sector.

"The qualifications and the demands are now such that the leadership is changing, the background is more educated and worldly," Santillan said.

Those interviewed stressed that they want to use this expertise to solve California's problems.

"We're going to be involved in transportation, technology, economic development," said 46th District Assemblyman Louis Caldera, a Democrat who is a West Point graduate with degrees from Harvard's law and business schools.

They are a diverse group, but among those interviewed, one commonality emerged: All strove to distance themselves from being seen strictly as Latino politicians. Not one ever once used the term "Chicano," preferred by the 1970's activists. The word has fallen out of favor over the more general "Latino." "Chicano" is now relegated to use mostly by academics.

"I do not see myself as a Latino politician in that this is the only community I represent," Caldera said. "You're only going to be relevant if you address issues of all Californians, not just one community."

At least one of the new assemblywomen, Diane Martinez, is even uncomfortable with stories (like this one) that single out Latino gains. Her being Latina is irrelevant and not worthy of mention, she said, and she downplayed it during the race. Martinez resents the seven Latinos in the Assembly being dubbed in some circles as *Los Siete,* after their number.

"I think that this is all journalistic racism," said Martinez, another Democrat and the daughter of Congressman Marty Martinez. "You never look at Anglos that way. It sounds like we're running in a gang. It's really very difficult to stomach to be treated as one of '*Los Siete.*'"

This distancing from ethnic roots caused a long sigh from longtime Chicano activist Raul Ruiz, who was in front of the bar on August 29, 1970 — the day Ruben Salazar was killed — taking pictures as the sheriff's deputy shot the tear-gas canister without warning. Ruiz, now a professor in the Chicano Studies Department at California State University, Northridge, stopped short of calling the new legislators *vendidos,* or sellouts, but he has been critical.

"They should say 'I am a Chicana,'" Ruiz said. "Often those who struggled the hardest are forgotten, and the little princesses and royal family members get these things bequeathed to them. They don't really deserve to get elected. What you saw elected here was the struggle of two machines, the Alatorre machine and the Molina machine. We do have some representation now. But in many ways the community is worse off. It's democracy, unfortunately sometimes with a small 'd.' The Black community has been served much better by the folks they elected into office. I'm much more im-pressed with the way they serve the community than ours do."

The past does weigh on many of the Latino legislators. For new Assembly members such as Martha Escutia, 35, the past is important — her experience, while perhaps not typical of all 10 Latino lawmakers, illustrates that simple labels do not fit the group. Escutia was the child of "firsts" in her family: first generation to be born in the United States, first to graduate high school, then college. In 1982 she graduated with a law degree from Georgetown. She is an activist, but not along the lines of the Chicanos who were in the streets during her youth.

"I came from a very conservative family," she said. "My family always told me, 'You're not Chicana, you're not Mexican-American. If you have to identify yourself as something, don't hyphenate yourself: You're either American or you're Mexican but you can't be both.' So I never related to the so-called Chicano movement, the *Movimiento.* When I was in college I was frankly too busy trying to do well academically and hold down 45 hours worth of jobs. I just had a different agenda. The agenda was I had to build the foundation in order to be successful, and after that I could become an activist."

Upon graduation, Escutia spent five hard years working in Washington, D.C., for the National Council of La Raza, then heavily involved with the 1986 immigration bill and other issues such as employment and training based on the German model of vocational education — a tough sell in the Reagan years.

Escutia feels the burden of "doing something." When interviewed not long before the November election, she was consumed with worry as she drove around her district that stretches from the southern tip of East Los Angeles through Huntington Park in the south. It is 88 percent Latino, and unlike East Los Angeles, which is now a settled community, has most of the new immigrants. Her district is California in a microcosm: dead factories, a lot of immigrants, gangs, poverty, crowded schools.

Escutia pointed out the poverty in plentiful supply — crowded apartments, jobless men milling about — and asked what she can do to change things in the face of monumental problems and a lack of money.

"I don't know how I'm going to do it. My ass is on the line," Escutia said as she gripped the wheel. But Escutia, an intense and passionate woman, is going to try. She feels that one way is to forge coalitions to work together instead of splitting over lines drawn by camps and ethnic groups.

"LA is on the verge of balkanization," Escutia said. "We're dividing into hostile groups. I resent that a lot of our traditional allies [are] fighting against each other. It's almost like piranhas."

The Black caucus is prepared to work with the Latinos, according to Democratic Assemblyman Curtis Tucker Jr. of Inglewood. The two ethnic groups will hold together now more than ever before, he feels, at least better than the Anglo West Los Angeles liberal legislators and their northern counterparts.

"We all want the same things," said Tucker. "We all want better education, affordable housing, health care, economic development. The difference in wants between the African-American community and the Latino community don't exist." 🏛

UPDATE: Cruz Bustamante (D-Fresno) was elected to the Assembly in a Special Election in 1993, increasing the number of Latino legislators to eleven.

GAY POLITICS

By J.S. Taub

Reprinted from *California Journal*, November 1993

It was a sticky, sweaty New York City night when the cops — on a routine prowl for vice — hassled the wrong crowd at the Stonewall Inn, a homosexual hangout in Greenwich Village. It was June 27, 1969, and the news hit the front page of the staid New York Times like a novelty on a slow news night. Whoever heard of a bunch of queers standing up to New York's finest? The Stonewall riot, as it is now known kicked off the modern gay rights movement.

Fast-forward one generation and the headline on the front page of one of San Francisco's gay newspapers reads, "It's here. The year of the queer. Get used to it." The last line was in three-inch type.

In less than 25 years, gays have struggled to replace the stereotype that characterized them as closeted, unhappy, incomplete, shadowy individuals with a proud and positive activist identity. This attitude fuels political action and organizations like Act Up and Queer Nation. And it was the force behind San Francisco's controversial "Year of the Queer" gay freedom day theme celebrating the 24th anniversary of Stonewall.

The gay rights movement hit an apex with President Bill Clinton's effort to end the ban on gays in the military. That, combined with increasing integration of homosexuals into business and the popular culture, has inspired more visible political action on civil rights, domestic partnerships, anti-discrimination and AIDS.

"Clinton's campaign for military service has had a direct effect," says David Mixner, Los Angeles gay activist and

---

J.S. Taub is a freelance writer from San Francisco.

---

adviser to the president on gay issues. "We were the fringe, a sideshow in politics. We raised the money but were kept at arm's length. Now we are in the mainstream. We delivered for him, and now we are being taken seriously as a civil rights movement."

For California's urban-based gays , the path to increased political clout is elective office and key appointments. This is a world of sophisticated party politics, political infighting, shifting loyalties, betrayal, strategy and sometimes outrageous action. Urban gays, especially in Los Angeles and San Francisco, have embarked on a full-scale integration into the political mainstream, bankrolling gay candidates, forming coalitions and, in some cases, severing past alliances.

Increasingly, gay men and lesbian politicos say that the era of reliance on straight allies in government to speak for gay issues is over and that gays must now advance to take their place at the political table and start representing themselves and other non-gay constituencies. Anything else, they insist, would be "plantation politics."

For many gays in California today, the issue is not simply holding hands in public. It's the threat of unemployment and violence and coping with the role AIDS has played in shrinking the gay political leadership and sapping creative sparks from the community.

What is gay political clout in California? Visibility is the apotheosis of the homosexual rights movement. For today's urban-based gays, "out" means not having to falsely manufacture a straight lifestyle. "Out" means openly acknowledging sexual orientation. "Out" means clout.

For some, "out" also means "queer." If one is not completely straight, meaning exclusively heterosexual, then one is queer, some say. And those same folks would advise gays and straights alike to get used to it.

Says Queer Nation co-founder Jonathan Katz, a professor of gay studies at San Francisco City College, "Queerness doesn't constitute a single identity because sexuality is fluid. Examine the investment the dominant culture has in marginalizing sexual expression. What do we do with someone who is married and has homosexual experiences? There are no neat boundaries..."

In California, some homosexuals feel they still lack total protection under the law because they are excluded from the civil rights umbrella covering women, minorities, the aged and disabled. A gay civil rights bill, AB 101 by Democratic Assemblyman Terry Friedman of Los Angeles, was vetoed in 1991 by Governor Pete Wilson, a moderate Republican who, during his campaign, had pledged support for such a bill. The bill would have added anti-discrimination protections of gays into the Fair Employment and Housing code.

Roberta Achtenberg

Nonetheless, another Friedman bill, AB 2601, was signed instead; it protects gays and lesbians against discrimination in the labor code. Another civil rights bill, AB 2199 by Speaker Willie Brown Jr., would restore a broad interpretation to the Unruh Civil Rights Act, which had been watered down by recent court rulings. Although a coalition bill, it is significant for gays because it would allow individual communities to establish more liberal anti-discrimination ordinances than does the state. A total of 17 California cities now have local anti-discrimination ordinances, including Berkeley, San Francisco, Los Angeles, Cathedral City, Cupertino, Oakland, Riverside, Sacramento, San Diego, Davis, Laguna Beach, Long Beach, Mountain View, San Jose, Santa Barbara, Santa Monica and West Hollywood.

A Gay Family Values Bill, AB 1581, also has been introduced by Oakland Democrat Barbara Lee, which would define domestic partners. Right now, only San Francisco, West Hollywood, Marin, Sacramento, Santa Cruz and Laguna Beach have enacted domestic partners registration, health-care benefits or other benefits for domestic partners of municipal workers. Domestic partners is a top priority for the gay community.

San Francisco and Los Angeles form a gay axis linking the southland to the north state. Northern California, with

Carole Migden

San Francisco as its flash point, remains a traditional center of leftist political action — home of the free-speech movement, hippies, the anti-war movement, the feminist movement. San Francisco gays wield hefty political clout within the Democratic Party. San Francisco homosexuals are among the most visible in the country, but it is a political community in transition and one that is beginning to recognize the diversity within its ranks.

"Part of the problem with the San Francisco gay and lesbian community is that it is very parochial, very tough," says Steve Kline, president of the city's Stonewall Gay Democratic Club.

"It's hard to break into the political circle if you didn't know Harvey [Milk] or you don't have his blessing. That's why radical activism and Queer Nation came into being. There is a generation gap, but there's a group that did not know Harvey." (Milk was the gay San Francisco activist who was elected to the Board of Supervisors, then murdered in 1978 along with Mayor George Moscone by former Supervisor Dan White.)

Moreover, while San Francisco's homosexual community is criticized by some as chaotic, Kline explains, "There was a breakdown among conservatives and liberals and different ethnicities and genders. We are a diverse community and we look for the homogeneous where there is none. In organizing you have to respect philosophical and ethnic diversity."

Nonetheless, Kline separates political influence from power and says the only way gays can build a power base is by electing gays to office. "We have to start electing our own. We can't rely on Mr. and Mrs. Straight no matter how liberal and progressive they are. They still don't understand what we have gone through, the process of coming out, of dying, the suicides. It's important for gays to be in the face of the Democratic Party; the Republicans don't let us in the room, the Democrats take us for granted. We need to be in their face more. At least we are being talked about," he says.

Nothing could illustrate gay clout in San Francisco better than conservative Mayor Frank Jordan's appointment of Susan Leal, a Latina lesbian health-care executive with no past experience in elective office, to Roberta Achtenberg's seat on the Board of Supervisors. Achtenberg was the first "out" lesbian to run for Assembly, a bitter campaign against now-Assemblyman John Burton, a gay rights supporter. She left the Board of Supervisors earlier this year to accept a post with the Clinton administration. "Appointing Susan Leal is recognition of our political strength," says Carole Migden, an "out" lesbian supervisor who chairs the board's budget committee.

Migden speaks for many gay Democrats who have accused their straight allies of taking them for granted. "The lesbian and gay community have been loyal Democrats and, as a voting bloc, our clout is unparalleled. But we have not been fostered, groomed, launched in the same way as other party regulars. We have not been picked out and pinpointed and assisted in the full range of our political potential," she says.

Assemblyman Burton argues that straight political allies are a big help. "It was straight politicians that legalized the gay and lesbian lifestyle, straight politicians that passed legislation to protect people with AIDS and HIV at a time when it was considered a gay issue," Burton says. "I don't subscribe to the view that you have to be a gay or lesbian to understand. Just like you don't have to be African-American to combat racial and economic injustice, or 70 years old to fight for the rights and dignity of senior citizens. That's their hang-up."

Indeed, betrayal can cut both ways, considering the significant loss of gay support for former San Francisco Mayor Art Agnos, a staunch advocate. "No one carried the rainbow flag in the straight community higher than Art Agnos," says Burton. "No one worked harder or more assiduously with the community. He introduced the gay rights bill while in the Assembly. He appointed gays to policy positions. But where did the opposition come from? It came from the gay clubs," says a perplexed Burton.

The answer, Migden says, is for gay politicos to develop their own alliances within the party structure. "That is the route to empowerment. We must take power. No one re-linquishes power."

Migden is highly involved in broad-based political issues. As chair of the board's budget committee, she spear-headed the debate with a concentration on salvaging funds for public health and AIDS, rape and crisis counseling, mental-health programs and drug-treatment centers. San Francisco's gay leadership is encouraging her to run for mayor in 1995. She is also being eyed as a possible replacement for Willie Brown when the term limits end his tenure in the Assembly in 1996. By then, Brown, Burton and state Senator Milton Marks all will be forced from the Legislature.

"Willie Brown's seat could be a gay seat," Migden says. "Originally with reapportionment, the Democrats had thwarted the interests of the gay community, but the boys in Sacramento gave that back. A lesbian or gay person would have an excellent chance to be elected to office in that Assembly district."

Burton, who refuses to confirm or deny reports that he is considering a run for San Francisco mayor, says, "I

John Duran

Robert Burke

wouldn't want to run against Carole."

If San Francisco is the heart of the gay movement, then Los Angeles is the power. San Francisco's soul mate to the south is wealthier, less ideological and more political. Angelenos are cool, strategic players under a self-imposed deadline to win political office by 1996. Southern California, influenced by the professional and entertainment industries, is not leftist, not politically correct and not ambivalent about money.

"LA has a different take on politics, and with San Francisco it's always how far on the left can you go. We represent the broad spectrum. We get smart, play hard ball, play votes and money," says John Duran, a West Hollywood civil rights attorney who was defeated in 1992 in a campaign for the 42nd Assembly District against incumbent Democratic Assemblyman Burt Margolin.

Money politics is exemplified by a fund-raising group called Access Now for Gay & Lesbian Equality (ANGLE), which raised $800,000 for the Clinton campaign and funnels money to gay and lesbian candidates and selected heterosexual candidates.

"Having other people represent your interest isn't acceptable," says Duran. "There have to be gays and lesbians on the finance committee, on the power commission, to be involved in the give and take of the political game. It's so easy for our allies to sell our issues down the river."

Los Angeles has a plan. With the redrawing of districts in the 1990 reapportionment, Los Angeles gay politicos predicted there would be no gays in elected positions beyond the local level. So in 1988, two years before legislative and congressional districts were to be redrawn, the Western Alliance of PACS conducted a survey to pinpoint who and where gay voters are and presented it to the Democratic Party leadership as evidence that they could win elective office. The reception was chilly.

And the angry response was swift.

"We ran a quick and dirty 90-day campaign against Margolin," says Duran. "We were running to lose, but lose well. They did not consider us as viable candidates because we were a special-interest group. We felt we were being taken for granted. We were angry. I ran against Margolin because the 42nd District had the largest concentration of gays and lesbians. We flexed our muscles and we carried the votes in the gay and lesbian precincts," Duran says.

Moreover, Los Angeles gays broke with their straight supporters as a result of a dispute with the "Berman-Waxman machine," an alliance between two Democratic congressmen from Los Angeles — Howard Berman and Henry Waxman — and their favored local politicians like Margolin,

Terry Friedman, Barbara Friedman and Herschel Rosenthal. Gays rallied support for Tom Hayden in his 1992 Senate primary against incumbent Rosenthal as a payback for promises that straight politicians broke, Duran says. As a result, Hayden squeaked into office.

In the November 1992 election, gay politicos put together a slate mailer sent to targeted gay households. "The results were overwhelming," says Duran. "It was a model. Any community could do this."

But the gay community wasn't strong enough to muscle mayoral candidate and ally Michael Woo into office. First, the vote was split. Richard Riordan, a conservative Republican, captured an estimated 28 percent of the 5 percent of Los Angeles residents who identified themselves as homosexual, according to a *Los Angeles Times* poll.

Bob Burke, the now openly gay political director of Riordan's campaign, had run and lost a bid for Democrat Mike Roos' old Assembly district in Silverlake in a 1991 special election. Party support for his opponent — now-Assemblywoman Barbara Friedman — as opposed to its promised support for a gay candidate for that seat, played a big part in the dispute between gays and the Berman-Waxman Democrats.

But Burke feels that despite the gay community's embrace of Woo, the candidate's support was lukewarm. "Mike could have taken stronger positions on an AIDS coordinator or trying to get a gay police commissioner. His administration was lacking in tangible results. We never got anything of substance," Burke says.

Gays do not perceive Riordan as anti-gay, just unpolished. "Riordan is not homophobic," say Lorri L. Jean, executive director of the Gay and Lesbian Community Services Center of Los Angeles. "He was elected as a fiscal conservative and anti-incumbent."

While Jean is optimistic about Riordan, she admits, "He doesn't know our issues. He makes *faux pas*. He didn't know AIDS Project Los Angeles, he pressed people's buttons by telling them some of his best friends are gay. He has some polishing to do," Jean says.

If gay Democrats feel frustrated by half-baked support from the Democratic Party, they are light years ahead of their counterparts in the Republican Party, which put on a National Convention starring famous gay-bashers Pat Robertson and Patrick Buchanan. But gay Republicans exude an all-American spirit that believes that if you do the right thing, and don't push your sexual orientation in their faces, that you will be accepted as a Republican who happens to be gay.

The Republican Central Committee wishes they'd go away.

The Log Cabin Federation is the main gay Republican political organization in the country. There are nine Log Cabin clubs in California. Founded in Los Angeles in 1977, Log Cabin members are liberal Republicans. Often their families have voted Republican for generations and they are fiscal conservatives in favor of a strong defense. They

also advocate that government get off the moral warpath against homosexuality.

"We are the element in the coalition that is fighting the religious right, but the problem is that there are very few Republicans in urban areas. The liberal communities acted as magnets," says Chris Bowman, political consultant and past president of the Log Cabin Club in San Francisco. Bowman says the reason gay Republicans are so weak is because "all of them became Democrats."

But gay Republicans are a durable minority. Bowman says Republicans are busy organizing in Ventura, Riverside, San Luis Obispo, San Diego, Sacramento and Kern counties. "Because gay power is concentrated in urban areas, we are not able to reach middle America. We will never be the majority, so we must organize in suburban and rural areas," Bowman says.

And Log Cabin takes some credit for rounding up the 28 percent gay vote that helped put Riordan on the mayor's throne.

Frank Richrazzi

Phil Perry, press secretary for the Republican leadership in Sacramento, expresses the mainstream Republican take on gay issues: "I don't care what the story is. They don't like the lifestyle, they don't want to hear about it. That doesn't mean they are Nazis and that they want everyone to stay in the closet or die of AIDS."

"Hard-core conservatives believe that government doesn't have a right to know what you do, but don't try to impress me with it. Don't be separate. No special protections. We should all just be equal and keep it to yourself. Don't throw it in my face," Perry says.

Gay Republicans agree. "We are not activists. I was elected to serve on the city council, not to be the gay advocate," says Wayne Peterson, an "out" gay who serves on the Laguna Beach City Council. A tiny pocket within arch-conservative Orange County, Laguna Beach, an artist community, has a large gay population. "I make my statements by setting a good example," Peterson says.

This is okay for most Republicans, says Perry. "Ninety percent of gay people fit in. They don't bash people with their lifestyle. But to the 10 percent that make all the noise and spit on cops and dress in leather and spikes, we say, 'Do we want to do something better for you?'"

Republicans blame Wilson's last-minute refusal to sign AB 101 on the bill's sponsor, Democratic Assemblyman Terry Friedman. "This is an issue that's five years old and that's where the consciousness is," explains Perry. "Pete was reminded of political realities ... and political pressure from his constituency. He ... doesn't like to be backed into a corner and browbeat. Friedman browbeat. Pete would have taken some amendments. Friedman would not take amendments. Friedman was the reason he didn't sign."

Perhaps. But backing out on his promise also set his loyal employees to grumbling. While quick to praise the governor for three openly gay appointments to the state bureaucracy, Frank Ricchiazzi, assistant director of the Department of Motor Vehicles, says, "There was a lot of anguish with that veto. He was our governor, we put him there. We put so much effort in getting votes in the gay community. We felt betrayed. We were the angriest of the whole community."

The real enemy, say observers, is homophobia — the negative feeling some homosexuals have about their own sexual orientation, and the open hatred and stigmatization of gay people by the religious right wing. This group never ceases its crusade to oust gays and lesbians from schools and churches and to promulgate its own Christian brand of pious intolerance.

"One area where we will be working together in a coalition is on domestic partners," says Laurie McBride, executive director of Lobby for Individual Freedom and Equality (LIFE), a Sacramento-based gay lobbying group that specializes in AIDS and civil rights. "A lot of heterosexual people want domestic partnerships and want to set up an arrangement. People will see that as an alternative system that values relationships in a strong and powerful way. Family is our most important issue. There will be a lot of family issues in the next five to 10 years."

McBride, however, acknowledges the strength of the opposition.

"We are attacked by the rabid right wing, the ayatollah of Anaheim," McBride says about the Reverend Louis P. Sheldon, chairman of the Traditional Values Coalition (TVC), an Orange County-based lobbying network of right wing Christian congregations. "I have had his people tell me they would like to throw the first stone at my execution. These people want to force us into a mold and keep us busy with surface issues of right and wrong," she says.

Christine Kehoe

The religious right wing is mobilized to make sure that every gain made by the gay community is met with a loss or the threat of one. Sheldon says the TVC is preparing a ballot measure for November 1994 to ensure that the civil code specifies marriage to be restricted to male-female relationships only. Two court cases, one in Hawaii and the other in California, seek to end the ban on same sex marriages on the grounds of gender discrimination. In the Hawaii case, the burden of proof is now on the state to prove there is a compelling reason for same-sex marriages not to be legalized.

State Senator Tim Leslie, a conservative Republican from Carnelian Bay near Sacramento, has proposed a Senate Constitutional Amendment, SCA 18, which would strictly define family as a man and a woman related by marriage, and a parent and his or her natural or adopted children. Domestic partners would not be recognized. Sheldon insists the TVC isn't being homophobic or bigoted when it describes homosexuality as perverted. "... We are standing up for family, and they are promoting a lifestyle that will destroy the culture, the family and western civilization.

"Homosexuality and perversion destroyed ancient Rome and ancient Greece. You have to keep the genie in the marital bottle. Men with men and women with women will destroy the culture..."

In addition to messing up the natural order, homosexuality, to Sheldon and his followers, is a health hazard. "With AIDS, we have come to see that homosexuality is a high-risk health factor," Sheldon says. "With AIDS and other sexually transmitted diseases, you can't keep yourself bodily clean. That's true with prostitution also. We haven't legalized prostitution."

As a gay political power emerges as a force, and as the community's political sensibilities mature to form coalitions with other groups struggling for representation, observers say gay issues will naturally fold into the interests of other minority groups, and that being gay will be yet another element of political diversity, like race or ethnicity. Thus, gay and lesbian politicians will be elected because they represent a broad range of interests. Some, like Democrats Jackie Goldberg of Los Angeles and Migden of San Francisco, are representing them now.

Meanwhile, those borders are being extended in bits and pieces by other, local candidates. But both Christine Kehoe, running as the first "out" lesbian candidate for the San Diego City Council, and John Laird, former two-term mayor of Santa Cruz and the only openly gay candidate for the California Assembly, ran coalition campaigns. "I broke the barrier in 1983 by being elected mayor. But that means I have a responsibility to be 200 percent better on government issues and service to our constituency. We have to be real," says Laird.

An aide to Councilman John Hartley, Kehoe is well known for community involvement and picked up endorsements from Hartley, who has decided to leave office, his supporters and the Democratic Central Committee.

The Kehoe coalition consists of small businesses, gays and lesbians, grass-roots neighborhood folks and a Republican city council member. She says her victory is important for gays and lesbians.

If being a gay officeholder is distinct from being a straight one, then being a lesbian officeholder is distinctive in a different way, says Migden. Lesbians are the part of the women's movement, which has a wide historical political outreach, and lesbians will thus be a major force in propelling homosexuals into the political mainstream.

Meanwhile, as term limits approach in 1996, gay candidates will have an historic opportunity to run for open seats in the Legislature. "When there are more open seats, there are more opportunities to fill those seats, and the more able gay and lesbian leaders there will be. There are numerous, outstanding gay and lesbian candidates," says Assemblyman Terry Friedman. "Those openings are opportunities for those who are prepared and ready to take advantage of that activity. It will happen for them if there is unity in the community." 🏛

Bye-bye, GOP. Ta-ta, Dems.

California voters flee traditional parties

Reprinted from *California Journal*, November 1993

Illustration by Chris Van Overloop

By Chris Collett

A favorite topic of debate among political pundits, pollsters and politicians over the last few years has been the question of whether California is more Republican or Democratic in its partisan beliefs. Without much question, it is agreed that the 1970s wasthe decade of the Democrats. In the fallout from Watergate, Jerry Brown was swept in for two terms as governor, and the Democrats built staggering majorities in both houses of the Legislature.

The 1980s, many then argued, belonged to Republicans. Bolstered by the California-based presidency of Ronald Reagan, a two-term governor in George Deukmejian and seat gains in the Assembly, the GOP overtook the Democrats in partisan identification for the first time in 1986. Presumably, as its supporters and some non-partisans have strongly argued, the only thing that kept Republicans from winning majorities in the Legislature and in the state's congressional delegation was

Chris Collet is a PhD candidate in political science at the University of California, Irvine.

gerrymandered districts. By 1987, Secretary of State March Fong Eu had warned her fellow Democrats that "California had become a Republican state."

With this in mind, it seems natural to ask, "To whom does California belong in the 1990s?" Recent election results suggest that the Democrats have re-emerged. Victories in two crucial U.S. Senate races in 1992, and stunning gains in congressional and Assembly seats despite districts more favorable to Republicans suggest that the Democrats, indeed, may be regaining the strength they enjoyed before the Reagan Revolution.

But the answer to the question, surprisingly, is that the decade of the 1990s seems to belong to neither Republicans or Democrats. The '90s, rather, are poised to be the decade of independents, decline-to-states and an assortment of third parties. Beginning in 1968, California steadily drifted from the two major parties, to the point where, in November 1992 (see Graph 1), nearly 14 percent of its voters were registered either as decline-to-state or with one of the state's minor parties. In terms of raw numbers, decline-to-state and minor-party registation have grown at whopping rates of 566 percent and 145 percent respectively since 1968. By comparison, Republican registration has grown at 62 percent and Democratic at 58 percent over the same time period.

Some would argue that in the candidate-centered age of politics, party registration means very little. In fact, recent research by Ed Constantini and Charles Dannehl at the University of California, Davis, has underscored this, by showing the decline in the relationship between Democratic registration and Democratic vote share in California.

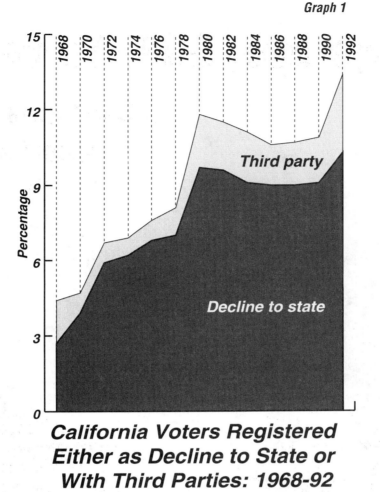

Graph 1

California Voters Registered Either as Decline to State or With Third Parties: 1968-92

source: Secretary of State, Report of Registration 1968-1992

Furthermore, registration data have been considered suspect because it is thought that one to two million voters still on the rolls are "deadwood" — those who have either moved or are deceased.

But the gradual movement away from the two major parties in the last 25 years is evident in the more trusted party identification data as well. Since 1966, *The Field Poll* essentially has asked respondents: "Generally speaking, do you think of yourself as a Republican, or Democrat, or what?" As Graph 2 shows (see page 33), the increase in those who give responses other than "Democrat" or "Republican" has steadily increased from 4.4 percent in 1966 to 33.7 percent in 1992. Like minor-party and decline-to-state registration, this trend reached its peak in last year's election.

While arguing that some sort of

enduring shift in partisan loyalties took place in California in the mid-1980s in the direction of Republicans, scholars of California politics such as Constantini, Kay Lawson of California State University, San Francisco, and James Fay of CSU, Hayward, have acknowledged this turn toward independence as manifested by shifts in registration data. But often, as noted above, survey data regarding party identification are cited to support the Republican cause, and indeed the data do support this case. Republicans have made considerable gains. But if party identification data are looked at in terms of the number of voters supporting neither major party rather than in terms of Republicans versus Democrats (Graph 2) we see a trend much more long term and dramatic than any recent shifts in partisanship.

Because California voters have become increasingly independent, such drastic shifts from Republicans in the late 1980s to Democrats in 1992 are not only possible but very likely to reoccur. Since independents — who again comprise anywhere from 15 to 33 percent of the vote depending on how one looks at it — are more susceptible to short-term electoral factors such as economic conditions, campaigns, and advertisements which influence the vote, elections may boil down solely to which campaign spends the most, has the most potent message, and makes the fewest mistakes. Democratic and Republican labels, even in legislative elections, have clearly diminished in value. "Coattails" have become non-existent.

California's move away from Republicans and Democrats is perhaps most apparent by recent trends in voting for

The independent voter

Graph 2

Percentage of California Voters Identifying with Neither Republicans nor Democrats

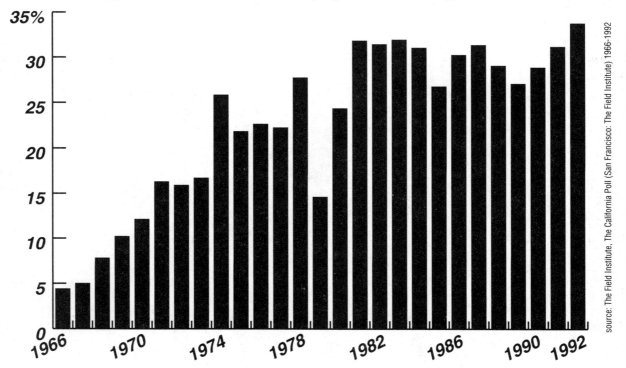

source: The Field Institute, The California Poll (San Francisco: The Field Institute) 1966-1992

third parties. In 1968, when the American Independent and Peace and Freedom parties emerged as the right- and left-wing alternatives to centrist politics during the Vietnam War, voters in California gave minor party candidates for the Legislature and Congress an average of just under 3 percent of the vote. This increased to nearly 6 percent in 1980, when the Libertarian Party first qualified for the ballot and fielded an entire slate of candidates. By 1990 the average share given to third parties had mushroomed to nearly 7 percent, and passed this mark in Assembly and State Senate races in 1992.

Voting for third-party candidates in statewide elections has also increased substantially. In last year's U.S. Senate races, all third-party votes combined accounted for 7.8 percent in the race between Democrat Dianne Feinstein and Republican John Seymour and 9 percent in the dust-up between Democrat Barbara Boxer and Republican Bruce Herschensohn. In the presiden-

tial race, gadfly independent Ross Perot gained 21.2 percent in the Golden State, which was above his national average.

The question, of course, is whether this increased share of the vote is enough to affect an election. While third parties still are not likely to win any legislative or congressional seats, they still may have an impact on given races. And in recent years, they have definitely impacted several incumbent and aspiring California politicians, including:

•Doug Bosco, a four-term Democratic member of Congress representing the North Coast, who was defeated 43 percent to 42 percent in 1990 by Republican Frank Riggs. Considered by many to be the upset of the year, it was widely held that the Peace and Freedom candidate, Darlene Comingore, who won 15 percent, split the left vote and kept Bosco form retaining his seat.

•Sunny Mojonnier, a four-term Assembly Republican from the San Diego area, who lost by 5 percent to Democrat Dede Alpert in 1990 in a

predominant Republican district. While ethics problems and campaign gaffes cost the once popular Mojonnier, Libertarian candidate John Murphy took 11 percent of the vote, and perhaps a close re-election from the Republicans.

• Jeff Marston, another San Diego Republican, lost what was considered a potential Republican seat to Democrat Mike Gotch. In a race that separated Marston from Gotch by 617 votes, Libertarian candidate Ed McWilliams garnered over 5000 votes, or 6 percent;

•Democratic Congressman Richard Lehman, who narrowly retained his seat in 1992 after being challenged by Republican Tal Cloud. In a race that was decided by less than 1000 votes, Peace and Freedom candidate Dorothy Wells received 12 percent, or over 12,000 votes;

• Republican Phil Hawkins who in 1992 challenged incumbent Democratic Assemblyman Bob Epple in the 56th District in Cerritos. Losing to Epple by 1 percent, Hawkins saw Libertarian candidate Richard Gard receive 5 percent of the vote.

• Senator Bill Craven, a Republican who has served in the Legislature since 1973. Running for re-election in 1990 free from a Democratic challenge, Craven still saw over 33 percent of the total votes go to the Peace and Freedom and Libertarian candidates.

In the fall of 1983, John Simon wrote in the *California Journal* that "in only a few cases, does one [of the third parties] hold a balance of power in a legislative or congressional district." But clearly, times have changed. An average of 7 percent — again, the average share given to third parties — was greater than the margin of difference between Republicans and Democrats in 13 legislative and congressional races in 1990, and 18 races in 1992. In total, these 31 seats were distributed nearly evenly to both parties, with Democrats winning 16 and Republicans 15. Thus, if third parties fielded candidates in these competitive, "swing" districts, they could now play a significant role in who wins the seat, and ultimately in determining which party controls each house of the Legislature and the congressional delegation. Because third-party candidates in Assembly races attract a slightly higher average vote share than do their counterparts in state Senate and congressional elections, their impact would likely be the greatest.

Whatever their impact on elections, third parties provide a constant receptacle for disgruntled Californians to cast protest votes. This may be an apt metaphor as a ballot cast for a third party candidacy is often considered a "wasted" or "throwaway" vote. But with an unpopular governor and Legislature — combined with increasing anxiety about the economy, education

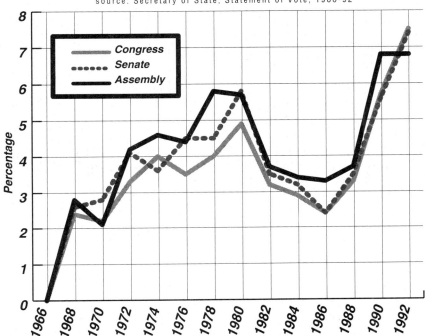

Graph 3

Mean Vote Share for Third Party Candidates in Legislative and Congressional Elections: 1966-92

source: Secretary of State, Statement of Vote, 1966-92

and immigration — the third-party phenomenon in California may be the latest channel of revolt for the politically disgusted. Call it the next chapter in an evolving California story that began in 1978 with Proposition 13 and continued through 1990 and 1992 with stringent term limits and cutbacks in legislative perks, services and salaries.

Equally plausible, however, is that third parties will become a fixture, if not a force, in California politics. No one is suggesting that there will be any Green members of Congress anytime soon, or any Libertarian members of the Assembly. But as long as the aforementioned conditions persist — weak party identification, sluggish economy, dissatisfaction with a government run by both parties — third-

party candidates will continue to attract many voters looking for alternatives. This creates an unpredictable scenario in many districts, especially in north coast areas where the Peace and Freedom Party and Greens have done well, and in Orange and San Diego counties where the Libertarians have prospered. Furthermore, given the trends in statewide party identification and registration and the current electoral climate, it wouldn't be that farfetched to see a Ross Perot or other independent slate of candidates emerge in California politics.

A small path along that route already has been forged by two members of the state Senate — Quentin Kopp of San Francisco and Lucy Killea of San Diego. Both are independents, with Kopp having originally run for the Legislature as an independent and Killea having left the Democratic Party in 1992 to run for re-election as an independent.

Finally, it should be remembered that California has traditionally been an independent state, with a long history of weak parties, non-partisan elections, a knack for quirky and sometime fringe politics and a fondness for eccentric politicians. Where else but California could figures such as Ronald Reagan, Jerry Brown, S.I. Hayakawa, B.T. Collins, Tom Hayden and others garner such attention? The California electorate today is as volatile as ever, and far from moving in one direction or the other as some have argued, it is likely to go both ways, and may, in fact, continue to search for an alternative route. 🏛

DIRECT DEMOCRACY

In California government the people have three tools that make them very powerful participants in the decision-making process. The initiative, referendum and recall were instituted by Governor Hiram Johnson and the progressives in part to break the hold of the railroad interests on state government in the early 1900's. With all three of the direct democracy devices, a simple majority of those voting determines whether the proposal passes.

• *Initiative.* The initiative gives the people the right to place local or state measures on the ballot if they obtain the required number of signatures. It has also been used by governors, legislators and special-interest groups to get what they want after the Legislature has rejected or been unable to meet their demands. To qualify for the ballot, a statewide constitutional initiative requires signatures equal to eight percent of the vote cast in the last gubernatorial election; initiative statutes require five percent.

After the 1990 gubernatorial election the number of signatures required is:

Constitutional initiative - 615,957
Statutory initiative - 384,973

Today, a powerful and sophisticated initiative industry has developed: signature-gathering firms, pollsters, political lawyers, and campaign management firms specializing in the qualifying and passing of ballot measures.

• *Referendum.* This is a procedure that can be used by the public, if they can gather sufficient signatures, to block a state statute or local ordinance pending a popular vote on the issue. It is not used often, but the threat of a referendum occasionally has the effect of blocking enactment of legislation. This procedure cannot be used to stop urgency bills, and for this reason emergency measures require a two-thirds vote rather than a simple majority in the Legislature. The referendum procedure was used successfully at the state-wide level to place four measures the Peripheral Canal and three reapportionment plans — on the ballot in June 1982.

The number of signatures required is the same as for a statutory initiative.

• *Recall.* The third of the Johnson direct-government reforms establishes a petition procedure for placing on the ballot the question of removing any elected official or officials from office. Recall elections are common in local government but have never been employed successfully at the state level in California.

California's system of direct democracy does not stop here. The Constitution and local-government charters can be amended only by a vote of the electorate. Neither the state nor any local governmental agency may incur a general-obligation debt without prior approval of the electorate (although revenue bonds can be sold without such approval). At the state level, a simple majority vote is sufficient to approve bond measures for such purposes as higher-education construction, park acquisition and development, the Cal-Vet farm and home program, and water-pollution plants. But at the local level, all bond proposals — even school bonds — require a two-thirds majority.

In recent years, the potency of direct democracy in California has grown. This power was demonstrated by the far-reaching tax revolt, which started with Proposition 13, the Jarvis-Gann property-tax initiative in 1978. This was followed with the "Spirit of 13" spending-limitation measure enacted in 1979, a successful Jarvis-sponsored income-tax indexing proposal in June of 1982, the successful Gann Legislative Reform Initiative of June 1984 and a number of other Proposition 13 follow-up measures thereafter. Proposition 140 imposes term limits on California elected officials, plus it mandates a 38 percent cut in the legislature's budget. Proposition 164 imposes term limits on our U.S. Senators and Members of the House of Representatives. The number of measures qualifying for the ballot shows no sign of abating in the near future.

With these tools, there is hardly any aspect of state government that cannot be controlled by the people. 🏛

Signing for fun and profit:

the business of gathering petition signatures

illustration by Wendy Rudick Shaul

BY CHARLES M. PRICE

Reprinted from *California Journal,* November 1992

Well, they're back. After a brief respite from initiative politicking in the June 1992 primary, a small platoon of signature-qualified propositions invaded the November 1992 ballot (Propositions 161-167). While dozens of initiatives were launched by hopeful proponents, only these seven made it.

Why did they succeed where all others failed?

Professional petitioning.

The seven were all jockeyed to ballot status through the efforts of California's only two "out-in-the-streets" signature companies: Kimball Petition Management of Los Angeles, and American Petition Consultants of Sacramento.

All it would have taken for the failed initiatives to qualify was money. Had their backers the money to hire Kimball or American, their proposals, too, would have reached the ballot. Qualifying initiatives using only volunteer activists and shoestring budgets is very difficult. Qualifying an initiative is expensive and lately seems to be the exclusive province of the well-heeled. For instance, according to the secretary of state, 80 percent of the money raised to qualify November's seven initiatives came from contributors giving more than $10,000. (Not only that, the first petition measure to qualify for the June *1994* primary ballot — the school choice or 'voucher' initiative — also used paid petitioners.)

The qualified initiatives and their professional petitioners are:

Charles Price is a professor of political science at California State University, Chico, and a frequent contributor to California Journal.

Prop	Title	Signature Company
161	Assisted Death	American
162	Public Employees Retirement	Kimball
163	Snack Tax Elimination	Kimball
164	Congressional Term Limits	American
165	Budget and Welfare Reform	American
166	Health Care	Kimball
167	State Taxes	Kimball
???	School Choice	American

Brothers Kelly and Fred Kimball Jr. are managing partners of Kimball Petition Managment, which their father founded in the 1960s. While Fred Senior was an arch-conservative who helped qualify many right-wing issues for the ballot (for example, Proposition 6 of 1978, which would have allowed school districts to fire homosexual teachers), Kelly and Fred Junior have shifted their company's ideological focus to more mainstream and even some liberal issues. Thus, in November 1992 the Kimballs worked on petition campaigns for Democratic-leaning interest groups such as state employees, the Tax Reform Association and the California Teachers Association. Since the late 1960s, Kimball has qualified dozens of petitions for state and local ballots.

American Petition Consultants also is the province of two brothers — Mike and Bill Arno. Mike is president, while Bill serves as director of operations. Their firm has qualified mainly Republican-conservative issues over the last decade, however American did qualify the liberal-leaning "Death with Dignity," for this fall. Said Mike Arno, "Philosophically,

I'm opposed to [Proposition 161], but it's a social issue that ought to be decided by the people, not the Legislature."

Despite the fact that they are competitors, competition in the signature-gathering business is not quite like competition in the personal computer business. And the links between the Kimballs and Arnos go back many years. Mike Arno's wife grew up as a neighbor of the Kimballs in Southern California. She persuaded Fred Senior to give Mike his first chance in petitioning as a crew chief for Kimball in the early 1980s, and he learned the business well. Over the years on a few occasions, when deadlines are imminent, Kimball and American have sometimes subcontracted with each other for a certain number of signatures. They've been friendly competitors — until this year.

Clearly, Kimball and American dominate initiative qualifying these days. Between 1982 and 1992 nearly 75 percent (48 of 65) of all of the initiatives on the California ballot have qualified through the efforts of one or the other of these two companies. Once hired, they virtually guarantee their clients' ballot status (each has a nearly a 100 percent success rate). Both firms also earn considerable sums qualifying initiatives in states like Oregon, Nevada, Washington, Michigan, Ohio, Oklahoma and Colorado. And, since the collapse of Communist rule in Eastern Europe, each firm has done consulting work in the newly emerging democracies there. Indeed, another Arno brother, Peter, runs their company's St. Petersburg/Moscow operations, and plans are afoot to establish a new office in Minsk.

Paid petitioning wasn't always needed to get a measure on the ballot in California. In the early years, after the initiative was placed into the state Constitution by reformist Progressives in the 1910s, qualifying could be handled by volunteers because proponents had 150 days to collect fewer than 50,000 signatures — a number based on a certain percentage of the total vote cast for governor at the most recent election (5 percent for a statute; 8 percent for a constitutional amendment).

But as California's population increased massively during the Great Depression and after World War II, collecting and processing the hundreds of thousands of signatures needed within the 150-day circulation period became a logistical nightmare — hence, professional petitioning. And since 1990, when the Colorado Supreme Court refused to review a lower court decision that states could not ban paid petitioning because it limited free speech, paid petitioners have truly come into their own.

Through the early 1980s the paid petitioning process went something like this:

• Kimball or American is contacted by an initiative proponent, and the two sides would settle on a price for collecting a specified number of paid signatures — 100,000 or 200,000, for example, with the remainder usually gathered by volunteers.

• The measure then is submitted to the attorney general's office, which assigns it an official title and summary and looks over the text to make sure it's above board and legal. The attorney general laterals it to the secretary of state's office, which assigns circulation and signature-verification deadlines.

• Thousands of copies of the petition are printed and sent to the Kimball or American crew chiefs around the state.

• Crew chiefs hire reliable solicitors by contacting people from previous campaigns and by advertising for new

ones in the classifieds.

• Crew chiefs brief their solicitors on a summary of the main arguments for the initiative and point them toward the best places to find signatures — for instance, shopping centers or where people are waiting in line.

• Crew chiefs also teach solicitors how to persuade a reluctant prospect by saying, "This doesn't mean you agree. It's just to get the measure on the ballot so the people will have a chance to vote on it."

• Solicitors turn in their signatures, receiving 25 to 35 cents per name. Crew chiefs earn 5 to 10 cents for all signatures collected in the city or area.

• Finally, proponents turn their accumulated signatures in to local county clerks for validation and tabulation.

Although paid petitioning in the 1990s follows a similar procedure, there are some interesting new twists in the business.

• **Independent subcontractors:** In the old days, American and Kimball had loyal crew chiefs who worked only for one or the other. But no more. As American's Mike Arno noted, "Today, our crew chiefs [located in most of the state's larger cities] are independent subcontractors. In the old days, we hired a lot of 'mom and pop' operators; for example, housewives who ran petition drives out of their homes. These days our subcontractors all have their own businesses. We try to buy the best contractors available.

"Sometimes, they're ones that have done a lot of Kimball work. These people are free agents and negotiate their best price. So, too, the solicitors are independents. A crew chief says, 'I'll give you 35 cents per signature,' and a solicitor says, 'I want 45 cents, or I won't do it.'"

Moreover, Kelly Kimball noted, "If you're slow in getting signatures, you've got to raise the price for the solicitors. It's a stock market out there. Some circulators will delay turning in their signatures on one of the petitions they're carrying, assuming the price will go up. It never goes down. We raise the price [per signature], and suddenly thousands of signatures come in. They bought low and sold high."

• **Multiple petitions:** To make money in petitioning these days, Kimball and American must have packages of three or four or five initiatives — not merely a single initiative — to entice the best petition subcontractors to work for them. George Gorton, Governor Pete Wilson's campaign manager who was spearheading the governor's budget-welfare reform initiative qualifying effort in 1991, failed in his attempts to negotiate contracts with petition subcontractors. The subcontractors want packages of initiatives because the more petitions, the more money and the better enticement for successful solicitors. In addition, subcontractors prefer to do business with known quantities. Wilson's forces eventually sought out Arno to collect the signatures for what has become Proposition 165.

Said Kimball: "There is no limit to what these people [solicitors] can carry."

Arno, in a similar vein, added: "The most petitions I've ever seen one solicitor handle was 13. He had every initiative ... on an ironing board. People would walk along the board, and he'd say, 'Are you for this one? ... Sign here. This one? ... Sign here. This one?' Some solicitors can make as much as $30 or $40 dollars an hour. Several have made $50,000-$60,000 in a five-month period."

• **Initiative awareness:** Before 1978 and Howard

Jarvis' property-tax slashing Proposition 13, the initiative process was not well understood by most interest groups. To attain policy objectives, these groups preferred to concentrate on lobbying and providing campaign contributions to candidates. In the 1990s, however, those same interest groups (and elected officials, as well) are keenly aware of the initiative option, and of the ability of Kimball and American to collect hundreds of thousands of signatures.

However, neither Kimball nor Arno say they try to talk people into filing an initiative — usually. Kimball acknowledged that he put together the Lottery initiative as a pro-active effort. "We were looking for something we could make money on, and somebody who would fund it," Kimball said. "But, there are just too few issues out there like that."

• **Validation:** Another difference between paid petitioning today and yesterday is that the two companies place much more emphasis on collecting *valid* signatures. As Arno explained, "Each of us have computers with lists of all registered voters, and we can do random-sample verifications of signatures brought back by our solicitors. As the petition business has developed, subcontractors don't want to get a reputation for turning in poor work. If they fall below our quality control standard, I can back charge them."

• **Direct mail:** In the early 1980s it looked as if direct-mail companies might supplant street petitioning as the wave of the future. Direct-mail petitioning still is used to supplement some petition drives, but it isn't the main signature source these days. Kimball, more pessimistic than Arno about direct-mail petitioning, warned that direct mail "just flat out doesn't work very well. It worked for Howard Jarvis, and it worked somewhat for [Paul] Gann, but on a limited basis. Many of the people on the Jarvis lists were not young, and some have since died. A direct-mail piece is tremendously expensive. If you don't get a decent contribution return rate, you're spending $10 to $15 to $20 per signature."

• **Motivations of initiative proponents:** On the contemporary scene, initiatives are no longer proposed simply as a last resort by interests failing to get their way in the Legislature. These days some issues are introduced via the initiative process. In addition, some initiatives dealing with the same issue on the same ballot are designed to confuse voters rather than to be approved. Some initiatives are put on the ballot to siphon money from conservative Republicans or liberal Democrats. As a result, the process has become more complicated and Byzantine.

• **The attorney general:** Finally, according to Kimball, the present attorney general, Republican Dan Lungren, has been exceptionally partisan. "The [initiative] summaries his office does contain his political philosophy. They're like campaign literature for the opposition." For instance, attorneys representing proponents of Proposition 167 (the so-called "tax the rich" initiative) had to go to court to get the attorney general's "partisan" summary modified. American's Arno, however, disagrees with Kimball's assessment.

It is still possible for dedicated activists to qualify initiatives in the 1990s, but doing so is a formidable undertaking. Perhaps, the prototype of the idealistic cause/volunteer of petitioning is Ken Masterton of Masterton and Little of Bolinas. Over the last few years, Masterton has directed successful qualification efforts for four different environmental initiatives for the Planning and Conservation League (Proposition 70 of June 1988; Propositions 116 and 117 of June 1990; Proposition 130 of November 1990). In addition, he was successful with Proposition 99 of November 1988 (the tobacco-tax) and Proposition 134 of November 1990 (the alcohol-surtax). While more emphasis is placed on getting volunteer signatures in Masterton's efforts, on most of his petition drives some paid signatures also are collected (indeed, two-thirds of the signatures he collected for Proposition 130 were paid). In addition, to secure his freebie signatures, Masterton must pay coordinators to organize the volunteer solicitors, and it costs thousands just to print all the petitions that will be needed. According to Masterton, the typical volunteer effort to place a statute on the ballot will cost about $250,000 to qualify. Thus, initiative qualifying, even those using mostly volunteer signature collectors, is expensive.

Relations between American and Kimball have cooled recently. The reason: the controversy over the qualification effort for the school-choice, or voucher initiative. Arno was hired by the initiative's proponents to collect the necessary signatures to place the measure on the November 1992 ballot. However, in a unique counter-strategy move, the California Teachers Association hired Kimball as a consultant to work *against* qualification.

"Our strategy in the anti-qualification campaign was to arm the potential signer with the information needed to say 'no,'" said Kimball. "If a well-educated teacher can explain why an initiative is bad to potential signers, this can be very effective. It wouldn't have worked to have our circulators do this. Teachers were ideally suited for it."

Arno, not surprisingly, saw it differently. "On the one hand, you had teachers who saw the choice initiative as a 'life or death' issue and, on the other side, you had people trying to earn money collecting signatures. Many of these people were in agreement with the philosophy of the choice initiative. It's a very frustrating thing to have someone jump in your face when you're trying to collect signatures. We had reports that potential solicitors were offered money not to get signatures, or were threatened if they tried to do so. They used Kelly to locate where all of our people were. If we fail to qualify an initiative, this obviously benefits Kelly."

Both Arno and Kimball are supportive of some reforms to improve the initiative process. Kimball noted, "If it were in my power, I'd really enforce the single-subject rule. I'd also like the system reformed so that voters would be asked a simple question, 'Do you want a state lottery? Yes or no?' And, if a majority of voters say 'yes' then the Legislature would be required to implement the law. We should not have to have voters wade through 20 pages of legal text describing an initiative. People don't have the time or energy for this. My proposal would be a sort of an indirect initiative."

But Arno wants the process to continue. "When I'm invited to speak to college classes," he said, "I always ask this question: 'Were there too many initiatives on the last ballot?' ... 'Which of them would you have like to eliminate from the ballot?' There is always much disagreement on this. 'How many bills were considered by the Legislature last year?' Most think a few hundred. I tell them, 'More than 6000. Can you name five of them?' And, they can't. But they know what the initiatives were. Finally, I ask, 'Who do you trust more — you making the decision or your legislator?' Overwhelmingly, *they* want to make the decision." 🏛

initiative reform

Is it time to return to the "indirect" initiative?

Illustration by Mike Tofanelli

By Charles M. Price

Reprinted from *California Journal*, April 1994

If public attitude toward state government was a radar screen, the little blip marked "confidence" probably has disappeared from view. And the reasons for it are myriad. Corruption unearthed in an FBI sting operation conducted inside the Capitol ensnared legislators, lobbyists and staffers. The economy has been blistered by defense cutbacks, an unemployment rate higher than the national average, a tidal wave of illegal aliens, a never-ending series of fires, floods, drought and earthquakes, and human maelstromes such as

the Los Angeles riots. When dealing with all of this, political institutions often seem mired in gridlock and unable to cope.

Thus, the public took matters into its own hands, using a process of "self-government" established more than 80 years ago — the initiative. Beginning with Proposition 13's overhaul of the property tax system in 1978, voters systematically restructured state political institutions and changed forever the way state and local governments funded themselves. They also put a cap on the amount of time state elected officials may serve in office.

But a growing number of critics feel that the initiative process, set up to curb the influence of special interests on government, has become instead a tool for those interests. Critics also feel that the laws that emerge from the initiative

---

Charles Price is a professor of political science at California State University, Chico, and a frequent contributor to California Journal.

system are flawed. And they want the process overhauled.

The initiative — together with its cousins, the referendum and the recall — first saw the light of day in California back in 1911 when Progressive Governor Hiram Johnson led the charge to write them into the state Constitution. Initiatives allow voters the right, via the petition process, to propose and enact laws and constitutional amendments, and, by so doing, bypass the Legislature and/or governor.

Initiative critics, including elected officials and academicians, point to a number of problems with the current system.

• Initiatives are often authored by special interests or by ambitious politicians, not by average citizens, as Johnson intended.

• These measures are filed and approved for circulation without any in-depth analysis. Although the attorney general makes sure proposals don't violate the constitution, many slip into circulation with drafting errors or are flawed in other ways that must later be sorted out in court.

• Most initiatives qualify for the ballot through the work of professional petition firms rather than the efforts of volunteer citizens.

• Initiative propositions are laden with legalistic jargon, making them difficult to understand for the average voter.

• So-called "counter-initiatives" — two proposals on the same subject and the same ballot — often complicate the voter's ability to sort among conflicting measures.

• Initiatives add to the length of the ballot and number of decisions facing voters.

• Propositions are packaged into deceptive campaigns by slick professional campaign consultants.

• Finally, initiatives, once approved by voters, are amended with great difficulty.

Beyond these problems, a succession of fiscal initiatives have severely hampered the governor and Legislature's ability to provide fiscal leadership — or even craft a budget. Included in this group are Proposition 13's 1978 property tax relief; Proposition 4 of 1979, which imposed government spending limits; Proposition 6 of 1982, which abolished property and gift taxes; Proposition 62 of 1986, which required a two-thirds vote before cities may raise taxes; and Proposition 98 of 1988, which mandated a minimum funding level for K-14 public schools.

Finally, voter adoption of Proposition 140 in November 1990, the harsh term limits and legislative budget reduction initiative, was for many legislators, especially Democrats, the "last straw."

Thus, over the last several legislative sessions, various Democratic legislators have proposed "reforms" to stem the initiative tide: raise the filing fee from $200 to $1000, require that signatures be collected in a specific number of counties, increase the percent of signatures needed to qualify an initiative or require that the percent be geared to registered voters not to the total vote cast for governor at the last election, the current requirment. This proposal would double the number of required signatures (currently 615,958 for a constitutional amendment and 384,974 for a statute). Yet, none of these proposals passed even though Democrats had secure majorities in both houses.

Restrictions on the initiative process fail for a number of reasons. First, conservative Republicans are wary of under-

cutting a process they often have used with great success. Term limits, for instance, was proposed by former Assemblyman and former Los Angeles County Supervisor Pete Schabarum — a Republican conservative. Second, polls repeatedly show that the public supports the initiative process. And although that support has declined over the last several decades, it still is backed by more than 60 percent of the electorate, according to *The Field Poll*. Third, an alliance of interests united to help protect the initiative during the 1991-92 legislative session. This "Initiative Coalition" included political watchdogs such as Common Cause and the League of Women Voters, environmental groups such as the Planning and Conservation League and the Sierra Club, and conservative anti-tax groups such as the Howard Jarvis Taxpayers Association, People's Advocate (founded by the late Paul Gann), and Paul Gann's Citizen Organization. The coalition opposed restricting the initiative process because its members had successfully sponsored initiatives and were reluctant to see the process dismantled. Moreover, the Jarvis and Gann groups have used the initiative process as a money-making tool to help fund their activities.

One significant initiative reform emerged from the 1991-92 session, however — Democratic Assemblyman Jim Costa's ACR 13, which established a 15-member Citizen's Commission on Ballot Initiatives to study the process and propose possible remedies. Under ACR 13's provisions, the governor, Assembly speaker and Senate Rules Committee each selected four members, with appointees a reflection of the state's diverse population. The commission also included a designee of the secretary of state, attorney general and president of the County Clerk's Association. Retired Legislative Analyst A. Alan Post, one of the most respected former officials in the state, was selected to chair the commission.

The commission met periodically during spring 1993 to listen to various initiative experts recommend initiative reforms and to formulate a proposal. Two experts in particular played key roles in framing the commission's deliberations: attorney Robert Stern, former counsel to the Fair Political Practices Commission and author of "California's Fourth Branch of Government;" and Floyd Feeney, a University of California, Davis, law professor and co-author of "Improving the Initiative Process: Options for Change." The "Initiative Coalition" also provided input.

In the end, the initiative process gained a vote of confidence from the commission, although there was substantial consensus that it had some problems. As Post commented, "I don't think that commissioners felt the initiative process should be constrained nor that it was overused. The intent was to make it a better instrument." Post and his colleagues agreed a comprehensive package of initiative reforms was needed and, in January 1994, they presented their recommendations to the Legislature. Costa packaged these recommendations into an omnibus initiative reform bill introduced in February 1994.

The most dramatic change proposed by the commission involves reinstitution of a modified "indirect initiative." Currently, initiatives that qualify go "directly" to the next statewide ballot. The commission would detour those measures by requiring that qualified initiatives first go to the

Legislature for evaluation.

Under an "indirect" system, sponsors of an initiative would have 180 days (30 more than under the current system) to circulate petitions and gather enough signatures to place their proposal on the ballot. But instead of going before voters at the next statewide election, the proposal instead would be sent to the Legislature, which would have 45 days to act on it. Lawmakers would hold hearings where proponents and opponents could testify. Lawmakers also would negotiate with sponsors to iron out flaws or correct drafting errors. Sponsors then could amend the measure as long as the amendments were consistent with the "purposes and intent" of the original proposal. Each house would vote on the initiative and — if the Legislature passed and governor signed it — it would become law without going before voters. The governor and Legislature also could adopt their own law on the same subject, and proponents could choose to withdraw their proposition if satisfied with the effort. If, however, the governor and lawmakers reject a qualified initiative, it automatically would be placed on the next statewide ballot, where it would become law if approved by voters. If a statute, the Legislature subsequently could amend it after three years by a two-thirds vote of each house. Constitutional amendments could not be amended by the Legislature.

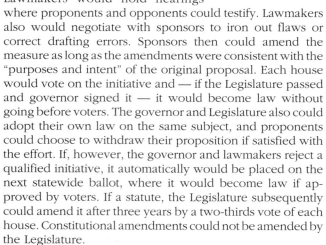

There are advantages to this approach, the commission argued. For one, proponents would have a little more time to qualify their petitions, and this might encourage more volunteer rather than paid signature collecting. More important, it would provide a mechanism for revising initiatives after they have been filed. Today, qualified measures go on the ballot, period. The commission's plan, however, would allow for hearings, complete with bill analyses, review and amendments. Oversights, ambiguities and gaffes in the initiative text could be corrected. For example, opponents of Proposition 165, sponsored in 1992 by Governor Pete Wilson to reform welfare and the budget process, focused on one significant drafting error: Although the proposal gave the governor emergency fiscal powers, the Legislature was not given the power to override his decisions. George Gorton, Governor Wilson's initiative campaign manager, admitted to the drafting flaw but contended the courts would take care of it. This could have been avoided had the commission's format been in force because Wilson would have had the opportunity to amend his proposal.

There are problems with the commission's recommendations, however. Hiram Johnson sought a procedure that would bypass a gridlocked or special interest-dominated Legislature. The proposal puts the Legislature back in the loop. Also, from 1911 to 1966, the California Constitution included both a direct and an indirect initiative, but the latter device was rarely used. Finally, *The Field Poll* reported in 1990 that 50 percent of Californians opposed the indirect initiative, while only 41 percent favored it. Also, if initiatives never reached the ballot, it would mean less money-making opportunities for campaign consultants.

In addition, opponents often want proposals killed, not amended, and see their best chance at the ballot. In this vein, they might not want to tip off proponents to drafting errors

at a legislative hearing but would rather spring these shortcomings on proponents later in the campaign.

The Post Commission also included a smorgasbord of other fine-tuning reforms, including additional contribution disclosure statements, improved signature-verification procedures, better ballot design, and full disclosure of the top five contributors to the proposition.

The commission, however, did not deal with the role of money in the initiative process. Court rulings mostly have preempted the subject. Powerful groups like the California Teachers' Association or the tobacco industry are in a better position to qualify their proposals than is, say, an animal rights' group because wealthy organizations can spend a lot of money on professionals to collect the required number of signatures. The U.S. Supreme Court ruled in 1988 in *Meyers v. Grant* that states can not prohibit paid petitioning because the ban limits free speech.

Clearly, the side with the most campaign money, particularly if it's by more than a two-to-one or three-to-one margin, has a better chance of winning at the ballot box. This advantage is even more enhanced in the 1990s because the "fairness doctrine" — which once required radio and television stations to provide some free air time to proponents or opponents of propositions with modest financial resources — is, at present, dead. Yet courts also have ruled that attempts to set contribution or expenditure limits also violate free speech.

The contemporary initiative process seems to work. Since the 1970s, only about 20 percent of the filed initiatives actually qualified for the ballot. Of these, only about one-third were approved by voters. If "too many" initiatives get on the ballot, or if initiatives are too lengthy or complex, voters tend to play it safe and vote "no." Thus, in effect, the initiative process already has a self-correcting mechanism.

For his part, Costa has pushed ahead with plans to author legislation to implement some commission recommendations. At the end of February, the Fresno lawmaker introduced AB 3181, which incorporates those recommendations that received unanimous support from the commission. Among the bill's provisions are the requirement for legislative hearings on proposed initiatives, a procedure for proponents to amend their measures, an extension of the circulation period, an improved signature-verification system, and provisions for additional campaign statements.

Costa also introduced ACA 40, which puts provisions of AB 3181 before voters. Both bills are headed for their debut before the Assembly Elections and Reapportionment Committee. Randall Henry, a senior consultant to Costa, expressed guarded optimism about the fate of the two bills, saying that Costa packaged only those recommendations that had been given unanimous approval by the commission, with its varied representation.

Still, Costa's success could depend on how lawmakers perceive declining public support for the initiative, legislative anger over term limits and support from the Initiative Coalition.

Meanwhile, the public seems to be in for a breather — the June 1994 ballot contains only one initiative.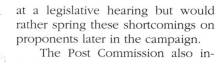

LOCAL GOVERNMENT

One reason why Californians have so many elections and frequently such long ballots is that the state has a complex system of local government. Every citizen in the state probably is a resident of a dozen or more units of local government, among them:

Counties. The state has 58 counties (counting San Francisco), some of which are governed by general state law and others by charters (similar to constitutions) voted by the people.

Cities. Most Californians live in one of the state's 468 cities, but many live in unincorporated areas in which municipal services are provided by the county and special districts. General law cities (384) operate through a structure established by state law. Charter cities have more flexibility in their structure and procedures.

City-county. San Francisco is a combined city and county operating under a charter.

School districts. Public schools from kindergarten through 12th grade are operated by independent districts with directly elected governing boards. There are about 1200 school districts in the state.

Community college districts. Directly elected trustees also run community colleges, which provide freshman and sophomore courses.

Special districts. These can vary from large regional districts such as the Metropolitan Water District in Los Angeles to a local mosquito-abatement district. There are more than 3,000 special districts formed to provide specific services for a defined area. Most directors are elected by the public.

Local Agency Formation Commissions. Each county has a commission that serves as clearinghouse for annexation of territory by a local agency and for formation of new cities.

Regional governments. There are no all-powerful regional governments in California, but there are numerous limited-purpose regional agencies such as the Bay Area Air Pollution Control District, Rapid Transit District and Sewer Service Agency. Efforts have been underway for years to enact a powerful regional government for the San Francisco area. There are several voluntary associations of local governmental agencies designed to help resolve regional problems; these include the Association of Bay Area Governments and the Southern California Association of Governments.

City and county government

Counties are run by boards of supervisors elected by the public, usually by district. In most counties, the board appoints an administrative officer to supervise the details of county government. Counties also have other directly elected officials, such as the district attorney, the sheriff and the assessor.

Cities are operated under a variety of systems. Under one basic arrangement not widely used, the strong-mayor system, the mayor is the chief-administrative officer of the city, and policy is set by the council. The more common system establishes the mayor, who may be elected either by the people or by the council, as the ceremonial chief of the city and puts the administration of municipal affairs under the control of a powerful city manager or administrator. The council has the power to appoint and remove the manager. Under this council-manager form of government, the council is supposed to be limited to the setting of policy, but there have been a few cases in which a mayor, by virtue of a strong personality, had been able to run the city government, relegating the manager to the role of errand boy.

More frequently, however, the manager, by virtue of the fact that he is a full-time employee with a large staff, plays a role as large as or even greater than the council in establishing policy.

Special districts are usually administered by a superintendent, general manager or other executive selected by the governing board. 🏛

Local government hits the wall

Proposition 13 finally comes home to roost

Reprinted from the *California Journal*, August 1993

By Mary Beth Barber

It's been 15 years since voters passed the property-tax-slashing Proposition 13, and this might be the year when its financial chickens finally came home to roost. The 1993 budget changes the way local governments earn revenue, shifting the emphasis from property taxes to sales taxes. Not only will this shift decrease their budgets in general, it may also affect how they view future growth. Some individuals, like Richard Gann (son of Proposition 13 co-author Paul Gann), claim that local governments will have to cut back and become more efficient. But budget critics like Democratic Senator Mike Thompson of Napa say that estimated savings for local government are grossly inflated. In addition, there will be some unfortunate long-term effects from the budget that he has dubbed "The Factory Outlet Act of 1993."

Since Proposition 13 first went into

effect in 1978, cities and counties have largely been spared the true ramifications of the measure, which limited the rate at which property tax could increase, by a state that provided them with compensatory money from other sources. The year Proposition 13 was passed, the state set this process in place through a bill known as AB 8 — the local bailout.

Everything went along smoothly until the 1990s, when California finally hit the recession wall and state government had to deal with serious budget shortfalls of its own. This year, in the third year of budget deficits, and politically unable to raise taxes, Governor Pete Wilson decided it was time to take money back from local government and, if locals complained, find alternative means for them to gain revenue.

Wilson and the Legislature had twice postponed that moment, first in 1991 when they agreed to impose a temporary half-cent sales tax, mostly to balance the state budget but also to continue to send money from property taxes to local governments. They managed to avoid big cuts to locals again last year. But by 1993, money going to cities and counties was at the very place where Wilson especially was looking for additional cash — the bottom of the barrel.

In the budget, $2.6 billion in property tax revenues will go to balance the state budget. To backfill for this loss, a half-cent sales tax imposed in 1991 and set to expire this past June 30th will be extended until January 1994. It may be extended past that date if voters approve it in a statewide election this November. In addition, cities and counties will supposedly save $535.6 million because the Legislature relieved them of having to fund certain state-imposed services. Workers' compensation reform is expected to save locals another $54 million. Finally, some other money has been funneled to locals from various transporation planning and motor-vehicles license funds.

Cities don't seem too upset by the deal. They, after all, are only being hit up for $288 million. It's the counties that are taking the brunt of the blow — a whopping $2 billion. The Wilson administration claims that most of that money can be gained back. Russell Gould, the newly appointed director of Finance and past secretary of Health and Welfare, pointed out that if all the counties support exten-

sion of the sales tax, they'll get $1.5 billion for their coffers. And with the law changes, estimated by the state to save $500 million, that just about brings them up to speed.

Counties, however, don't see it that way. They worry about the uncertainty. Even eliminating the state mandates doesn't mean counties can, politically, enact some changes, said Peter Detwiler, longtime consultant to Senate Local Government. The mandate relief list includes allowing counties to eliminate Medi-Cal optional benefits that the state drops, tells them they don't have to pay for school crossing guards, allows them to wait 72 hours instead of 24 hours to file a missing-persons report, and changes some county requirements for the mentally ill. Eliminating some of these would be political suicide for supervisors in some cases, said Detwiler. "You have to remember, mandates are there because somebody wants them" he warned.

Other complaints concern the time limits placed on some of the mandate relief options. Many of them only apply for one or two years, while the property-tax shift is a permanent measure, said Steve Swendiman of the California State Association of Counties. Others, such as a proposed two-tier retirement system, don't represent savings until five years down the line, but state budget-writers credit it with saving $100 million. "This is all smoke and mirrors," said Swendiman.

Thompson voted against the budget, claiming that the savings for counties are realistically closer to $50 million, at least when he looks at the counties he represents. Furthermore, relief from the mandates falls unevenly. Some counties might have savings, others might not.

Another sore point for counties is the lack of a guarantee voters will extend the sales tax in November. But Gould is confident that most counties will end up with the extension. If a county's board of supervisors ratifies the extension or the county's voters approve the extension by a simple majority, it will share in nearly $1.5 billion statewide. With such a scenario in place — that it takes the vote of the supervisors or the voters — chances are good that the measure will pass across the state, said Gould.

Local governments no doubt will

be grateful to get the extra money. But many question whether the taxing mechanism leads to the best long-term planning for a city or county. When property tax was the essential revenue source for a local government, planners encouraged residential projects and industry. But local officials speculate that cities and counties will encourage development of stores and shopping centers instead of housing and manufacturing because shops and malls produce sales-tax revenue. Housing and manufacturing chew up resources in services, infrastructure and maintenance, said Swendiman.

Currently, it's difficult to say exactly how all of this will affect local governments because there are no completed surveys or analyses, said Debbie Thompson of the League of California Cities. But she noted that even now some cities are basing their future development plans on the results of this year's budget, and favoring projects that will gain sales tax. Most observers point to the situation faced by the city of Monrovia. Originally intending to accept a bid from Kodak to build a small manufacturing facility, Monrovia officials apparently abandoned the Kodak proposal and instead prepared to build a Wal-Mart. Debbie Thompson claims that city officials felt they would be faced with budgetary problems with the Kodak facility, while the Wal-Mart would provide sales taxes. "They turned away $20 per hour jobs for part-time employment" below $10 per hour, she said. "And that doesn't help the economy in the area." Other cities could use similar reasoning in the future. "Obviously every city can't have an auto mall — that isn't realistic," she said. "But cities may tend to favor projects that get them sales tax."

Housing development could decrease as well, said Swendiman. Smaller or even middle-size residential areas don't support themselves because the property tax taken in doesn't fully support the cost to build and maintain such things as sewers, sidewalks and roads. "I think it will be a much more fee-driven system," he said. Low- and moderate-income housing will be driven away. Not that all local government officials will choose the sales-tax revenue route because all elected officials behave differently, said Swendiman, but the incentive to do so is far greater than before.

Gould, on the other hand, points out that cities and counties still get much of their revenue from property taxes, and the speculative "auto-mall theory" is just that — speculation. "I guess I'm not convinced that it's going to occur," he said, adding that planners aren't completely short-sighted when making decisions. The trade-offs in the budget package that allow local governments relief from state mandates far outweigh the speculative "auto-mall" theory, he said.

Carol Whiteside, director of intergovernmental relations for the Wilson administration, said that while the state was looking for the best solution in the short term, the shift may actually improve overall planning in the state. Rural counties in the north state are looking to combining duties to help revenue problems. "This is new — it's been pushed by the economic situation," she said.

Further, as property taxes become

less important, counties will have less incentive to build development projects

Thompson   **Swendiman**

in unincorporated areas. Counties have sought to develop in areas that were not incorporated into cities to gain the property tax revenues, resulting in projects springing up in the middle of rural land miles from other development. Take

away counties' incentive to build in this manner, and new development will take place where it should have in the first place — around existing cities. "Whether that is good or bad is relative," she said, "but we want to be cost-effective — environmentally and economically. Building in unincorporated areas is more expensive," in terms of money and environmental effects. Large areas of open land are much more environmentally sound that smaller ones broken up by housing developments connected by freeways.

Both sides agree that the next few years will be milestones for local governments as they reorganize how they gain revenue and how they plan development. The move wasn't planned very carefully, said Richard Gann. "They only acted when the state got into trouble," he said. "They should have been weaning off local governments for years." 🏛

Counties in revolt

Stung by a grab of property taxes by the state, county governments are fighting back

Reprinted from the *California Journal*, April 1993

By Danielle Starkey

The budget has been signed, the back-patting has subsided and legislators have scattered to their districts for the month-long summer recess.

But the dance isn't over yet, county officials have warned. Angered that the state is balancing the 1993-94 budget on a $2.6 billion property tax grab" from local governments, counties have vowed to continue the fight in the courtroom and at the ballot box.

"The state has now opened up the taxpayers' purse and is saying, 'We're going to play in your pocketbook,'" said Contra Costa Supervisor Sunne McPeak. "We think this is an improper thing to do and a stupid thing" for the state to dodge its responsibilities and force local governments to cut programs, she said.

Contra Costa is one of at least 22 counties that have adopted ordinances ordering their county auditors to defy the law and withhold property taxes from the state, and 36 counties have passed resolutions, supporting the retention of taxes, according to Daniel Wall, lobbyist for the California State Association of Counties (CSAC).

"Contra Costa County went one better: they put a measure on the ballot," Wall said, and 78 percent of Contra Costa's voters approved the measure, which calls on the county auditor to defy the state.

Whether counties have any force of law on their side is yet to be determined, but the state Constitution (Article XI, Section 1) clearly indicates that counties are subdivisions of the state and their powers are defined by the Legislature. According to Brad Sherman, chairman of the state Board of Equalization (which adjudicates tax disputes), the state has the authority to determine the distribution of property taxes, and auditors who refuse to comply with the law could go to jail.

But legal experts in Los Angeles County and elsewhere are not deterred. In addition to ordering its auditor not to hand over the money, Los Angeles County has sued the state over the tax shift, alleging that it violates the state Constitution, said Frederick Bennett, Los Angeles' assistant county counsel. Other counties — including Contra Costa, San Diego, Plumas, Sonoma and Kern — also are preparing legal action, according to McPeak.

Governor Pete Wilson and his allies — including Democratic Assembly Speaker Willie Brown Jr. — defend the tax shift as necessary to maintain education funding at current levels in the face of declining revenues. They say that if counties, which collectively stand to lose $2.2 billion from the shift (the rest comes from cities, special districts and redevelopment agencies) are successful in their efforts to withhold the money, not only will the budget be thrown off balance, but additional cuts in state services will be required as the state takes the equivalent amount of money from the state general fund.

Further, the shift is not a "tax grab," Wilson andBrown insist, but rather an end to a state subsidy California can no longer afford, and that counties have enjoyed ever since voters approved the property-tax slashing Proposition 13 in 1978. (Prior to Proposition 13, which capped property tax rates at 1 percent, local governments could set their own tax rates.) The formula for determining how much money is taken from each county under the tax shift is linked to the formula in the so-called county bail-out bill passed in 1979 that helped local governments survive the loss of property tax revenue, said H.D. Palmer, assistant director of the Department of Finance. Democratic enclaves such as Los Angeles and San Francisco appear to have fared worse than Republican enclaves such as San Diego and Orange counties (see chart above), but that is not politically motivated, according to Fred Silva, chief fiscal adviser to Senate President pro Tempore David Roberti of Los Angeles. "People try to divine motives and external forces at work here," such as that Pete Wilson was protecting San Diego, of which he's a former mayor. "But no, that's not the objective, it's the outcome. It happens that San Diego had a relatively low property tax rate because they'd been reducing property taxes before Proposition 13," he said.

*I*n any case, legislators and the governor agreed to measures to help soften the blow to local governments, Palmer said. These include extending until January a half-cent sales tax that was set to expire last month (a move Wilson agreed to after pressure from local law-enforcement officials); a reduction in state-ordered local programs and a ballot measure in November to give voters the opportunity to decide whether to make the sales tax permanent.

County officials say that some of the mandate relief is irrelevant, since they can't in good conscience stop providing certain services to their neediest residents. In addition, they say, voters may reject the permanent tax.

"I think it's really difficult to budget without knowing what your revenue stream is," acknowledged Democratic Assemblywoman Debra Bowen of Venice, who cast the deciding vote on the state budget last month. But she said that she worried her Los Angeles district could have been worse off under another budget scenario if she had stuck to her "no" vote.

The speaker has made no secret of his disdain for county complaints, and in particular has attacked Los Angeles County (which sent some high-powered contingents — including Supervisor Gloria Molina, a former assembly-woman — to Sacramento to convince legislators to strike a better deal for Los Angeles during budget negotiations). In an Assembly floor speech in which he labeled Los Angeles supervisors "scalawags," Brown said it was unconscionable for counties to complain about what amounted to a 1 percent reduction in their overall budgets when state government was being cut 7 percent.

"For openers, the Los Angeles supervisors never should have been in Sacramento making any requests. This Legislature, with regularity, has been overly generous to Los Angeles," Brown said later. He also has criticized Los Angeles for supporting a "bloated system" that pays supervisors $99,297 per year, and close to 450 additional county employees more than $100,000 per year.

Counties respond that much of their budgets are dedicated to state and federally mandated health and welfare programs. In Los Angeles, 87 percent of the budget is spoken for and 13 percent is discretionary, said Bennett.

"If [the state] is going to be intellectually honest about this, they need to look at the amount of money [counties receive that is] earmarked ... to state and federal health and welfare programs," said McPeak. "If they did that, you'd find it's more than their '1 percent' [cut to counties]. I don't know what that calculation is based on," she added.

*L*ocal governments are loathe to lose a share of property tax revenues because that has been a wonderfully stable source of income, said Rebecca Taylor of the California Taxpayers Association. "All of these local jurisdictions love the property tax. Until recently, the average annual yield of year-to-year increases has been in the double-digits," she said. The theory that a sales tax alone could make up for the loss of property tax revenue doesn't work for most counties, since they are "tax poor," she added.

Among the allegations in the Los Angeles lawsuit are that the state's taking of the property tax violates the constitution because under Proposition 13, the 1 percent property tax was to be allocated according to law, but didn't specify which law. Courts will be asked to decide if counties — or a vote of the people — take precedence over the will of the governor and Legislature in allocating those dollars.

Los Angeles also is attempting to show that the shift amounts to depriving counties of "home rule" since it deprives Los Angeles of such a substantial portion of its discretionary income. Finally, Proposition 98 sets forth a formula for counties and the state to contribute to education. "The state has now reneged on their position on education funding and has asked the local taxpayer to contribute more than is provided for in the state Constitution," said McPeak.

To Silva, these efforts will come to naught. "Counties are an administrative arm of the state, whether they like it or not. They don't have the same 'home rule' privileges that charter cities do," he said. In addition, the county has misinterpreted Proposition 98 — the initiative that guaranteed a certain level of spending for education. "What Los Angeles County is trying to assert, wrongly, is that the real test [for education spending under 98] is 40 percent of general-fund revenue and nothing to do with property taxes."

Wall said that a CSAC task force is investigating the feasibility of getting the Legislature to approve a constitutional amendment to prevent the state from reallocating the locals' property tax revenue. 🏛

Immigrant bashing: Good policy or good politics?

By Danielle Starkey

Reprinted from *California Journal*, October 1993

photo by John R. McCutchen, San Diego Union-Tribune

Gold Mountain."

That's how California was known in the late 1840s, when word of the gold rush spread across the Pacific to China. California was rural and sleepy at the time, but the discovery of gold at Swiss immigrant John Sutter's mill changed the course of its history. California became a magnet for a worldwide flood of immigrants.

The gold rush ended long ago, but the lure of wealth in the Golden State has remained constant in the imaginations of men and women who seek a better life. The "gold" is no longer nuggets panned from stream beds or torn from the earth; it is a job, the promise of a car, a house or three squares a day. For some, it is the freedom to speak one's mind.

But these days, the "gold mountain" image of a California seen from afar by would-be immigrants is at odds with the tarnished reality of a California seen close-up by its current inhabitants. They see a California of high unemployment, gridlocked government, shuttered military bases and jobs lost to other states; a California of inch-along freeways, overcrowded schools, explosive cities and slam-jammed prisons; a California fallen on hard times.

And they are restless.

Unfortunately, there are no quick fixes for California's hard times. The problems are complex and global, and the state's political system has become increasingly hard-pressed to come up with solutions. When times are good, no one complains about the influx of immigrants; no one complains when illegal aliens work in tomato fields, hotel kitchens and garment-industry sweatshops for sub-minimum wages, helping to keep California businesses competitive. But hard times bring with them an increasing urge to find someone to blame — a scapegoat. And as the tide of illegal aliens sweeping into California has quickened, especially from Latin America, the illegals find themselves in political crosshairs, despite evidence that their contribution to the state's current economic malaise may be less significant than politicians would have people believe.

Politically, however, illegals have little chance to move out of those crosshairs. They are an impotent constituency, wielding virtually no political clout. They don't vote and don't contribute money and thus represent easy targets for politicians heading into the 1994 election season. As a result, both Democrats and Republicans have been jockeying of late to see whose boot can be placed most firmly on the neck of illegal immigrants. Ideas that a year ago were condemned as racist and hysterical now have entered the mainstream, and erstwhile liberals are joining with conservatives on a number of proposals.

But just as some unusual pairings have taken place, there also have been some deep rifts created among traditional allies that may have lasting repercussions. For instance, some Latino Democrats have been growing more and more angry over what they perceive as immigrant-bashing by fellow Democrats to placate conservative elements within the party. Assemblywoman Martha Escutia, a newly elected Democrat from Huntington Park, recently warned that some Latinos are so furious with Democrats for pressuring them to support anti-immigrant bills that they have considered bolting the party and re-registering as independents. She said some of them already have passed that warning on to Democratic Party Chairman Bill Press. Not only that, but Latinos themselves are split on how best to address the issue.

"Right now, [the immigration issue] is equal to Proposition 13 in terms of its volatility among the voting constituency," concluded no less a political observer than Assembly Speaker Willie Brown Jr.

Governor Pete Wilson and most of the state's lawmakers agree that immigrants historically have come to this country in search of a better life, or a better-paying job. But they divide on how best to reduce the flow of illegal immigrants. Some, including Wilson, want to focus on the illegals themselves, to stop spending state money on them in the form of services such as education and health care. Others, including many Latino Democrats, want to cut off the supply of available jobs by shifting the focus to those who hire illegals.

For Wilson and many California Republicans, the key is the so-called "magnet" of free services that since 1986, states have been required to provide to undocumented residents. "Since the imposition of those mandates, the number of illegals coming into this country and into this state have absolutely exploded, and the cost of providing services as a result of these mandates has absolutely exploded," said Dan Schnur, the governor's communications chief.

According to the governor's office, in 1988-89, California taxpayers spent $22 million to provide emergency medical services — including labor and delivery services — to illegal immigrants, and $640 million to educate their children. In 1992-93, the state spent $367 million on medical care for undocumented immigrants and $989 million on education. Most of these children receiving an education are

U.S. citizens. Their parents may be here illegally, however.

"I think we should quit telling the world that they can come here and receive emergency health care" and other services, Wilson said in a recent interview. If the federal government isn't going to fully reimburse states for having to provide those services, as it is authorized to do under the 1986 Immigration Reform and Control Act (IRCA), the mandates should be lifted, he added.

*T*o help drive home his point — and at the same time score political points on the eve of his re-election bid — Wilson this past August took out ads in newspapers around the country, calling on President Bill Clinton to support a constitutional amendment denying citizenship to children of undocumented immigrants, and to end the mandates. Democrats were quick to denounce Wilson for being "political."

But Democrats, too, had been riding that same bandwagon. As one Latino legislator observed, "[Democrats are] trying to cushion themselves from the political hit pieces that will be coming out next year." Among the Democrats grabbing cushions this year were state Treasurer Kathleen Brown, a probable candidate for governor in 1994; U.S. Senator Dianne Feinstein, a candidate for re-election herself in 1994; and U.S. Senator Barbara Boxer. Their proposals — which included militarizing the border — angered many of their Democratic colleagues.

"The Republicans have made this a lightning-rod issue, and the Democrats have bought into it," grumped Assemblyman Richard Polanco, a Los Angeles Democrat who heads the Legislature's Latino Caucus.

Democrats may have bought into it, but they also lobbed a few grenades at Wilson's proposals on immigration. When the Wilson ad appeared, Democratic Party political director Bob Mulholland accused the governor of pandering to the GOP's right-wing at a time his approval rating was low. He also said Wilson was "flip-flopping" on immigration, since as a U.S. senator in the mid 1980s, Wilson wrote an amendment to IRCA "at the request of his agribusiness contributors" that was intended to continue the cheap supply of farm labor to growers and has resulted in the legalization of more than one million illegal immigrants.

Schnur retorted that Wilson has been sounding the alarm for years about the growing problem with illegal immigrants — some two million of whom have settled in California. He is on record, for example, in a November 1991 *Time* magazine interview, as calling for more federal dollars to help California.

"At that time, Pete Wilson was villified," Schnur said. "He was called a racist. He was called a bigot. He was called an immigrant-basher. They said he was dumping on the poor. Call it whatever you want, but when you're done with the name-calling, we still have a problem in this state." Besides, sniffed Schnur, Wilson's amendment was "hijacked" in the Democratic-controlled House of Representatives. His original amendment — for a guest-worker program that did not grant citizenship rights — was amended in conference committee. Then-Senator Wilson voted for the amended bill, however. Wilson himself jumped into the skirmish by inviting critics of his record to "kiss my rear end," if they could reach it.

Wilson's newspaper campaign also brought an immediate response from Latino lawmakers, who attempted to shift the emphasis away from illegals themselves and onto those who profit from them. Some of the Latinos' proposals overlapped Wilson's, and included stiffer penalties and asset forfeitures for convicted smugglers of illegal immigrants, extradition of undocumented immigrants convicted of felonies, beefed-up visitor tracking to stop visa abuse, and a call for Congress to disburse the $812 million promised to states that absorbed the majority of immigrants legalized by IRCA.

But the political complexities rife in the issue of illegal immigration surfaced starkly at an August press conference called by the Latino Caucus to unveil its proposals. That conference careened wildly off course when, in a rare moment of political honesty, freshman Democratic Assemblyman Cruz Bustamante, who represents an agriculture-rich region around Fresno, admitted under questioning that his district *required* illegal immigration.

Other Latino legislators standing with Speaker Brown in a semi-circle behind Bustamante visibly blanched. They looked at one another. They looked at their shoes.

They looked worried.

The competing imperatives — deny

services to immigrants or impose sanctions on those who profit from immigrants — had clashed not at a debate between Wilson and Bob Mulholland but at a press conference called by Latinos themselves. Although they had planned to discuss a set of measures that specifically did *not* include sanctions like asset forfeiture for employers who hire undocumented workers, the issue loomed into view once Bustamante broached the topic. Bustamante then said that asset forfeiture as a penalty on employers "would be devastating to the economy" of his district. Only moments later, however, Polanco said he would support asset forfeiture against repeat offenders. "It's ironic the politicians have stayed away from the employer sanction aspect of this debate," Polanco said, an apparent reference to the fact that it was much easier to go after powerless illegals than after often-powerful employers of illegals.

Bustamante's remark showed that even Latinos have trouble agreeing on a unified approach because the vested interests they represent are not monolithic. Bustamante also had demonstrated how difficult it will be to realize political gain from an issue that strikes so deeply — and often so divisively — into the notion of who we are, and where we come from.

Not that Bustamante wanted to hammer immigrants themselves. A former farmworker and the son of farmworkers, he tried to articulate the complexities by noting that everyone benefits from "the hard back-breaking work that I've done, that they [immigrants] still do, that none of you do, or ever will do." He argued that farms need a reliable labor source, but he also noted that most immigrants come to this country not to get benefits but to work. "We have to find a way to navigate through this immigration policy, to be able to provide our businesses an opportunity to continue to produce, and at the same time be able to allay the fears of people [that immigrants aren't coming to this country] solely for the reason of getting benefits."

It was left to Speaker Brown to lend some perspective to the conflict — and to call attention to the impact of asset forfeiture on business. "If it is determined that you have cavalierly hired [illegal immigrants]," Brown said, "you have violated the law to gain an opportunity for profit and you ought to have to forfeit the profit you've made. Of course,

my farm types [go] nuts about asset forfeitures for farm products [but] my guess is that [Disneyland] would never use undocumented persons again if you had forefeited the Matterhorn." Brown was referring to the federal Immigration and Naturalization Service recommendation that Disney pay a $394,840 fine for violating laws requiring documentation of workers' immigration status.

Conflict over how to deal with illegals, and the political skirmishes that accompany that conflict, were most noticeable during the waning days of this year's legislative session. Democrats pushed through a number of bills, including one by Palm Desert Democratic Assemblywoman Julie Bornstein that imposes state penalties and asset forfeiture for convicted smugglers of illegal immigrants. Another bill, by Los Angeles Democratic Senator Art Torres, transfers undocumented felons to the Immigration and Naturalization Service as soon as they are convicted. (see following story). And Santa Clara Democratic Senator Alfred Alquist authored a bill to require first-time driver's license applicants to show proof of legal residency. Alquist's measure proved one of the most controversial.

Republicans, meanwhile, focused on reducing the magnet of services. Assemblyman Richard Mountjoy of Monrovia, for one, turned up the heat during Assembly floor sessions by repeatedly introducing amendments to cut off public services for illegal immigrants. His amendments were routinely squashed by majority Democrats, but some observers saw them as attempts to put Democrats on record as voting against immigration reform. One of Mountjoy's efforts would have banned the use of state money to educate undocumented children, which required overturning an earlier court decision.

But not every proposal near and dear to Republicans was defeated, and at least one Mountjoy idea popped through — albeit, after being commandeered by Democrats. This was the Alquist bill, requiring first-time applicants for a driver's license to prove they are U.S. citizens or legal residents. It also allows drivers to get a temporary license while their residency is being verified and carries a warning that the license does not establish eligibility for employment, voter registration or welfare. If signed by Wilson, the law will take effect March 1, 1994.

The license bill highlighted conflicts brewing within the Democratic

Party and among Latinos. Proponents of Alquist's bill argued that it would stem the flow of illegals by making California less attractive to people who won't be insured to drive, and because a driver's license also is mistakenly used by employers to verify eligibility to work. Opponents countered that immigrants won't be deflected by the fact that they can't get a driver's license. More important, some Latinos feared that the proposal could lead to greater harrassment of people of color.

"If we're going to have that legend on the driver's license that it will not be used for employment, voter registration or services, then why go through the incredible document production to establish residency?" Escutia stormed during the floor debate on the bill. "In the final analysis, only people like me will be forced to show residency."

Escutia complained that the bill accomplished little in the way of substantive action and merely was designed to allow Democrats to tell their constituents that they had done something about the problem of illegal immigration. Not every Latino agreed with Escutia, however. In fact, Alquist's Assembly floor jockey was a Latino — Democratic Assemblyman Louis Caldera of Los Angeles.

Caldera initially opposed the bill, saying a license provided one of the few forms of positive identification, complete with a picture and address "of people involved in car accident with you." Moreover, not having a license could cause illegals to bolt the scene of an accident because "you just upped the stakes for them" if they are asked to show a driver's license and can't.

Caldera said he changed his mind on the bill because it looked as though it had enough votes to pass, and he wanted to be a player in the process to refine it.

"I think some of [my original concerns] are still legitimate," he added. But at least this bill "addresses the nexus between jobs and illegal immigration," since many employers still do not know that the driver's license is sufficient to establish eligibility to work. The new language on licenses will address that concern, he said.

The issue that seems most divisive for Democrats, and has created some unlikely alliances between liberal Democrats and Republicans, is sanctions against employers who hire illegals. Nearly all Democrats agree that illegals come to the U.S. seeking jobs, not health-care benefits or an education. "If there are jobs here that undocumented workers will take because they're willing to work for nothing, simply because nothing is more than what they're getting now, then you're going to continue to have that flow" of illegal immigrants, said Torres of Los Angeles, who supports sanctions.

Torres and others want to cut off the supply of jobs by enforcing federal sanctions against employers who hire undocumented immigrants. "The only person in America who is enforcing employer sanctions now is Bill Clinton," Torres added, referring to Clinton's rejection of cabinet nominees who had hired illegal domestic help.

But employer sanctions are anathma to Republicans because they hammer a traditional GOP constituency — the business community. Employer sanctions also make some Latinos nervous. Escutia, for one, worries about the impact of sanctions on *all* Latinos, not just illegals.

"I know that's a dual-edged sword for us as Latino Democrats to be arguing that, hey, we have to enforce what's already on the books — and that's employer sanctions — knowing damn well that by enforcing them we are leading down a path that will cause discrimination against people like myself and my community," she said. "There've been documented cases of discrimination because employers just don't know which documents [employees offer as proof of legal residency] are real or fraudulent. What ends up happening is they don't want to take a chance on hiring someone who looks like me and so they hire someone who looks like you."

Wilson said that the ease with which illegals can find very convincing counterfeit documents make employer sanction cases difficult to prosecute. "Under the present system," he said, "the law is largely unenforceable because, in fact, employers really cannot fairly be held to penalties because it's almost impossible for the INS to tell the difference, and they've got pretty sophisticated equipment."

Wilson said he might support some employer sanctions if California were made a test state for a federal, tamper-proof identification card that could be used for verification of legal residency. He's called on President Clinton to institute just such a test program in California. "If you have a card that is in fact tamper-proof ... it would certainly be fairer to impose tough sanctions on employers who, with the opportunity to

be protected by a tamper-proof card, ignore that," Wilson said.

One sanction Wilson is dead-set against is asset forfeiture. An asset-forfeiture bill sponsored by Polanco and Democratic assemblymen Tom Umberg of Santa Ana and Tom Connolly of Lemon Grove died on the last day of the legislative session but promises to be resurrected next year. It would give state and local law-enforcement agencies the authority now enjoyed by the federal government to enforce laws against those who hire illegal immigrants. Repeat offenders could lose equipment, research products and even records.

Wilson opposes asset forfeiture as "overly onerous," according to Schnur. The governor prefers to concentrate instead on ending federal mandates on states to provide services to illegals — a stance that makes some Democrats apoplectic. "Is someone asking ... if they would rather have [the] children out on the streets?" said Assemblywoman Hilda Solis, Democrat of La Puente.

Denying a service such as medical care raises issues of conscience and safety, as well as of cost. Health officials worry that denying care to illegals not only would be inhumane but could contribute to the spread of contagious diseases — thus, increasing costs to health-care providers. "You end up jeopardizing the whole community. Communicable diseases have no boundaries," said Polanco.

Wilson would not have doctors violate the Hippocratic Oath but rather have the "choice" whether to provide services. "What people are confusing is the absolute denial of services, which we are not proposing, with the lifting of the mandates forcing doctors and hospitals to provide health care services to illegals, which we are proposing," Schnur said.

Schnur noted that even President Clinton has indicated that undocumented immigrants will not be covered in his sweeping, national health-care reform plan, and said that Henry Cisneros, secretary of Housing and Urban Development, also supports denying government health and welfare benefits to undocumented immigrants and their families.

When asked how Wilson envisions mandate relief, Schnur acknowledged that the details are still sketchy. "But you would not deny educational services to a child, regardless of citizenship status, that had already begun the

educational process," he said.

Meanwhile, politicians of every stripe continue to propose ways to deal with the problem of illegal immigrants. Among those floated during the past year are:

• Tying passage of the North American Free Trade Agreement to treaties to ship home undocumented felons, who cost California taxpayers about $500 million per year. The idea, originally discussed by former Republican U.S. Senator John Seymour, now is championed by Kathleen Brown. NAFTA supporters oppose the idea because they fear that imposing additional side agreements to the plan could sink it.

• Imposing a $1 border-crossing toll to pay for beefing up border patrols — an idea pushed by Feinstein. State Department officials have warned that the fee could damage relations with Mexico and Canada, since it could be viewed as a restriction of commerce. They also say that the $400 million in anticipated revenues based on the number of crossings last year is optimistic, since travelers would consolidate crossings to avoid the fee, while others would try to cross illegally. Supporters, including Feinstein, note that international air passengers already pay a $10 fee to enter the country and say the money is badly needed for border patrols.

• Stationing National Guard troops alongside federal INS agents at the border, a proposal urged by Boxer. She was excoriated by Democratic colleagues, who accused her of militarizing the border, and Republicans such as Wilson, who said the idea doesn't make sense.

• Deporting undocumented felons.

• Cracking down on those who come here legally with a visa and never return home. In 1991 an estimated 317,827 visitors overstayed their visas.

The problems caused by the growing numbers of immigrants — both legal and illegal — are real, not some fabrication meant to create a scapegoat. But the scope of the problem is in dispute. What is not in dispute is that an election season is just around the corner, and immigration is a front-burner issue. For elected officials and candidates, the temptation is to apply rhetoric and blame to an inflamed situation — a tactic that could play well in an election year but exacerbate the already difficult task of devising substantive and lasting solutions.

And those solutions must be devised with one reality in mind: California will always be a gold mountain to the world's impoverished dreamers. 🏛

Crime issue knocks education out of the spotlight

Reprinted from *California Journal,*
February 1994

Laura A. Locke

Last November, many connected with public education in California were genuinely excited about the promise of 1994. The special election on the fate of Proposition 174, the school voucher initiative, had brought the state of K-12 education into a sharper political focus than it had enjoyed for several years. Despite the ringing defeat of their costly and controversial measure at the polls, voucher proponents reminded voters that there was work to be done in the state's schools. Opponents, victorious though they were, were forced to concede that the public's judgment was not a ringing endorsement of the status quo.

Within weeks of the voucher vote, everyone who was anyone in California's political elite weighed in on the subject. Governor Pete Wilson offered up a multi-point plan for school improvement on the very day of the election. His plan included retaining a hired-gun consultant (or, in Wilson's words, "education ambassador") named Dr. Frank Newman, who runs a Denver-based education think tank. State Treasurer Kathleen Brown, considered the favorite for the Democratic nomination for governor, also came up with a multi-point plan for school reform. Assembly Speaker Willie Brown Jr. announced he would convene an "education summit" in mid-February, modeled after 1993's successful "economic summit." In December, Wilson nominated corporate takeover specialist Sanford Sigoloff to fill the vacant post of state superintendent of public instruction.

What a difference a few months can make. As the solid defeat of school vouchers fades into the background, it appears education already is being eclipsed by crime and the state budget as issues of primary public and political concern. A measure of how far schools have slipped off the radar screen came in the governor's recent State of the State address: Education merited not one word of mention in a 35-minute speech. Administration officials said there just "wasn't time" during the speech, though the governor did find time to plug his "crime summit," then slated for mid-January but canceled after the Los Angeles earthquake.

"The educational system of this state is over half of the state's budget," said Democratic Assemblywoman Delaine Eastin of Fremont, the only announced candidate for state school superintendent. "I do not know how you can talk about the state of the state and fail to discuss what's going to happen in education. It's an outstanding omission."

• If school reform is to again fall through the political cracks, it won't be because it wasn't urgent enough. According to a survey commissioned by Policy Analysis for California Education (PACE), an independent education policy research group, nearly nine out of 10 Californians believe schools need to be changed, and more than two-thirds believe a complete overhaul is in order. The lopsided numbers are not surprising, considering the challenges facing this $30 billion behemoth.

- Of the five million-plus kids who attend school in California, more than a million are limited English-proficient;
- California ranks next-to-last among the 50 states in class size, and has spent time at the bottom of the heap;
- According to the National Assessment of Educational Progress, California students rank near the bottom in reading achievement;
- California schools spend nearly $800 less per-student than the national average, despite having to support the seventh-highest teacher salaries in the country;
- For the first time since the early 1980s, the proportion of high-school students taking the college-prep requirements for the University of California declined.

What makes school reform so elusive is that nobody can quite agree on the target. Terms like "education reform" and "restructuring" are continuously bandied about, but the terms mean different things to different people. Some reformers, like those who backed last year's voucher initiative, center their attention on the governance of schools and school districts. Reformers within the system — such as teachers' unions, administrators and school boards — tend to focus their gaze on finances (or lack thereof). Still others, particularly in the religious community, target curriculum reform as their top priority. "Reform" also covers such topics as revamped textbooks, educational technology and even self-esteem courses.

"Education is a conflict of values," said Michael Kirst, professor of education at Stanford University. "People want different things from the schools and reformers always want something different than what they are getting."

Semantic distinctions are not the only roadblocks to reform. Education has been polarized and paralyzed by a complex web of political agendas — sometimes interlocking, sometimes conflicting. In high-profile fights, such as those involving funding or last year's voucher campaign, key interest groups such as teachers and administrators band together, forming what's euphemistically described as "the Unusual Coalition." When it comes to the details of reform, however, these interests splinter and spin to reflect their own self interest. Talk to the California Teachers' Association, the state's largest teachers union, and you'll hear a lot of talk about the "respect" their profession deserves. Talk to the California School Boards Association, and you're likely to hear more about fiscal and professional "accountability."

Then there is the practical side of reform; in other words, how do you pay for it? The last three years have seen schools fighting just to keep the money guaranteed them by 1988's Proposition 98 school-funding initiative. For the past two years, Governor Wilson has kept education spending just above the Proposition 98 minimum funding level, in part by a series of "loans" against future funding. The CTA has challenged the scheme in court. Although there were no additional cuts in the 1994-95 spending plan, no adjustments were made for inflation or increasing enrollment demand on a system burdened with 150,000 new students who enter state schools annually. The CTA says that's a cut any way you slice it.

Add to this mix the additional complication of an election year. "We have a very politicized election for governor on the horizon, and maybe for superintendent of public instruction," notes Democratic Senator Gary Hart of Santa Barbara, chairman of the Senate Education Committee. "It's a very difficult environment to work in a neutral fashion when everybody is hyper and super-charged."

The rapid pronouncements about school reform that followed the voucher election, and the equally rapid disappearance of this talk once authorities found the body of Petaluma kidnap victim Polly Klaas speak to the ephemeral nature of political destinies.

"He [Wilson] has focused on crime as the tool by which he'll get himself re-elected," said Speaker Brown following the State of the State address. "There may be an attempt to overlook education, but we won't let that happen."

Brown's comments, of course, are viewed by some Republicans as disingenuous, given his own participation in a turf war that has paralyzed recent attempts at school reform from within. The battle itself started during the tenure of former schools chief Bill Honig, who was forced out of office in 1992 after being convicted on conflict-of-interest charges. Honig frequently locked horns with conservative Republican Governor George Deukmejian's appointees to the eight-member State Board of Education. The appointed board challenged the elected schools chief's authority in court and won a decision basically giving it broad latitude to shape not just curriculum but funding priorities as well. The court also gave the board confirmation power over four of the superintendent's appointed assistants, who would serve for a fixed, four-year term and could not be removed by a subsequent superintendent. Thus, the elected superintendent of public instruction was reduced to little more than a cheerleader for education, and when lightning rod Honig was grounded, there was no one left but caretaker David Dawson, Honig's assistant, to run the show.

Wilson tried to fill the slot last spring with state Senator Marian Bergeson, a Newport Beach Republican, but a searing opposition campaign, led by Eastin and orchestrated by Brown, overwhelmed the overmatched nominee. The post has remained empty, filled with the nearly invisible Dawson. Wilson's next proposed appointment to fill the void didn't help fill the "vision gap" — corporate takeover specialist Sigoloff, who was named primarily to serve as a structural handyman. He conceded no prior knowledge or understanding of public schools and no interest in running for the job this year.

It all seems so insurmountable that it isn't hard to see why reform has moved so slowly. In fact, with so many political crosswinds buffeting its docks, what's really remarkable is that schools can make any progress toward improving their quality. Yet, progress has been identified, primarily as a result of the last significant wave of reform. In 1983 the Legislature passed, and Deukmejian signed, Assembly Bill 813. The 214-page law offered 83 separate improvements, including tougher curriculum, broader testing, and a renewed emphasis on the basics. The groundbreaking reform effort, led by Honig and reluctantly agreed to by Deukmejian, was prodded by the release, in April of 1983, of "A Nation At Risk", the political firebomb lobbed by President Ronald Reagan's National Commission on Excellence in Education. The report has been defined by its cataclysmic rhetoric about "a rising tide of mediocrity" in the nation's schools that, if imposed by a foreign country, would be considered "an act of war."

Although progress has been hampered by the tightening budget screws, measurable improvement has occurred in several areas. The school year was lengthened to 180 days. Textbook protocols were updated, forcing publishers to upgrade the content of textbooks or risk losing out on a share of the lucrative California market. Statewide graduation requirements were implemented along with more vigorous model curriculum standards. Among the most significant achievements is the fact that the statewide dropout rate declined more than 30 percent between 1986 and 1992. Math and science test scores also have stabilized, particularly among middle school and junior high school students.

For those toiling on the ground in education, the most important future reform would be for the state to renew its commitment to the 1983 reforms. "The reforms are working and making a difference," says Susan Verne, a teacher for 20 years in south Sacramento County's Elk Grove School District. Verne's school, Florin High, is a microcosm of the challenges facing public education these days — 29 different languages are spoken among the students and the school has swelled from its design capacity of 1800 to now hold more than 2500 kids. Verne credits AB 813 with helping her classroom adapt to changing times, allowing teachers to move beyond the traditional role of lecturer to become "a facilitator." External resources, such as public television, newspapers, and periodicals, are welcomed into the classroom as supplements to traditional book learning. Verne also points to the holistic approach of the reforms, which emphasize establishing the school as a hub of the community.

"We have attempted to ... involve all of education's stakeholders: teachers, students, parents, business, and community leaders," says Verne. "This attitude wasn't here 10 years ago. When you bring the community into the school, you start to make a difference."

While they concede strides have been made, many education leaders insist schools are a long way from hitting the tape in the race for reform. "Not as much is happening as I would like to occur," says Hart.

What would Hart like to see happen?

For starters, more charter schools and broader public school choice. Hart has carried legislation in both areas, which share the common theme of introducing a competitive element into education. Charter schools are designed as individual self-contained entities, stripped of many of the more onerous bureaucratic constraints. The goal is to give professionals a chance to test different approaches — one might be strictly college prep, while another might be an arts and performance school. Public school choice goes even further, offering students and parents a chance to cross district boundaries in order to send their children to any school they wish, space permitting.

In the past, Hart's efforts have butted up against the education establishment, especially the CTA. The union, however, softened its opposition to charter schools and has even been less openly hostile to public school choice. Why? According to CTA president Del Weber, policymakers have sought CTA input as the reforms are being developed. "None of the [past] reform efforts have ever taken teachers out of the classroom and asked for teacher input," says Weber. "CTA has only been asked to react and respond."

On a more practical level, however, CTA's new tone may have less to do with a change of heart than a change of circumstances. In surveying its membership, CTA has found that the concerns of teachers extend far beyond salaries, fringe benefits, and protection of collective bargaining — the tradi-

tional union bailiwicks. Teachers are also desperately concerned about the conditions in which they operate. When it makes its case to the education summit, CTA will emphasize these aspects of reform, as well as those involving curriculum and funding. "It's in our best interest to have this work," says Weber, "otherwise we're going to have another voucher initiative on the ballot."

Ah, yes: vouchers.

The specter continues to haunt the education community despite having polled barely 30 percent support in last November's special election. True believers in Proposition 174 have remained remarkably undaunted by the magnitude of their defeat and are already loading up for another try. Some are pushing for a quick vote this November; three different voucher initiatives have been submitted to the secretary of state, including one by Terry Moe who, as a senior fellow at Stanford's Hoover Institution, is one of the concept's many fathers. All adhere to the basic concept of Proposition 174, calling for parents to be given a flat dollar amount that could be used to send their kids to the public or private school of their choice.

Moe's reworked plan addresses concerns that 174 didn't. It insures access by setting aside 15 percent of admissions for poor kids; protects Proposition 98 funding guarantees for public schools; and builds in accountability standards for private schools through curriculum, financial disclosure, testing and teacher qualifications. Moe wants to strike again while the iron is hot, insisting the distractions of election-year politics will keep the CTA from dumping the same $10 million spent last year to defeat Proposition 174.

"A quick turnaround is more advantageous for our side," Moe insists.

That view, however, is not shared by many others in the voucher movement, especially those who control the purse strings. "We will be back, but when, we don't know," said Kevin Teasley, who served as the key spokesman for voucher supporters during the campaign. Even Moe, despite his desire for a quick hit, concedes there are practical obstacles to another try this year. Moe, however, believes the very educational establishment that torpedoed vouchers last year will be the key to their eventual revival. "[They've] put out the fire, now they'll move on to other things," he says. Moe also dismisses the planned summit as being "all for show."

While Moe's derision is doubtless colored by his political zeal for the voucher concept, the despairing pessimism he expresses about public education is not so easy to dismiss. Education in California has been inventoried to death, and its flaws — both real and imagined — have been well documented in countless reports by task forces, blue-ribbon commissions and foundations. Yet, all that is offered by policymakers is more studies: an education summit here, an independent analysis there. Meanwhile, as the physicians argue over the right prescription, the patient's condition grows worse. Some suggest that, if the slide continues, education's role as a unifying democratic institution could collapse.

"Education is only one of several ways the state influences where we are going to be in the 21st century," says San Jose-based education consultant Patrick Callan. "If we fail to effectively make this collective investment in our kids, then California may no longer be conducive to being a prosperous and humane place. ⬛

PAY AS YOU GO

Privatizing California's "Public" Higher Education System

By Steve Scott

Reprinted from *California Journal*, March 1994

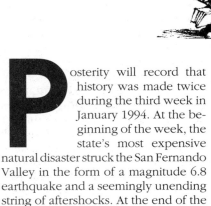

illustration by Christopher

Posterity will record that history was made twice during the third week in January 1994. At the beginning of the week, the state's most expensive natural disaster struck the San Fernando Valley in the form of a magnitude 6.8 earthquake and a seemingly unending string of aftershocks. At the end of the week, a different kind of aftershock tumbled out of a San Francisco meeting of the University of California Board of Regents. With only two dissenting votes, the 25-member board took an unprecedented step. They didn't admit that they'd taken it. The university's administration, in fact, explicitly denies that they've taken it. Nonetheless, by all but the most ephemeral semantic criteria, the University of California adopted a policy toward resident students that its founders would have considered unthinkable.

It began charging them tuition.

The barrier was crossed not when the board approved a $620 increase in "student fees" for the coming fiscal year. It wasn't crossed when they also approved a multi-year fee plan that could, by 1996, push UC student fees from the current $3700 a year to more than $5400 a year. No, the psychological line in the sand was erased with the adoption of an accompanying policy change which, for the first time, explicitly permits the use of student fee money to help pay "instructional expenses," including faculty salaries. The new policy effectively breaks the "no tuition" compact at the cornerstone of the 1960 Master Plan for Higher Education, which proposes fees only for non-instructional, "support" services.

"I don't care what you call it. We're charging tuition," says Ward Connerly, one of only two votes against the fee changes.

Not that the change comes as any great surprise. The definition of "support" services has broadened over the past decade and not too long ago was expanded to include money for libraries. For many involved with higher education, however, the change at UC is the clearest symbol yet of how far California has strayed from the public higher-education utopia of the Master Plan — accessible, affordable higher education for every adult who can benefit. Consider the following:

• Governor Pete Wilson's new state budget proposes a $7 per unit community college fee increase. If approved, full-time community college students will pay $600 a year, or about as much as it cost to go to a California State University campus just six years ago.

• Last year, the CSU Board of Trustees approved a four-year fee-increase structure designed to increase student fees to one-third the cost of instruction. If fully implemented, that means fees could rise as high as $2400 a year by 1997, or a four-fold increase in just nine years.

• Enrollment in public higher education in the state last year dropped by 160,000, or 8 percent, far and away the largest drop in the nation. Most of that enrollment decline was in community colleges, which lost 137,000 students.

• If the UC price structure approved by the regents is fully implemented, "fees" at the university in 1996 will be roughly three times what they were when Wilson took office in 1990.

"People have always thought in California that if you did the right things, and took the right courses, there was a place for you in higher education," says Patrick Callan, director of the California Higher Education Policy Center, a San Jose-based think tank. "We've put a damper on that."

The guardians of UC, CSU and the community colleges maintain the dramatic fee hikes are simply a reaction to the collapse of the California economy and to the shrinkage in state revenue available for higher education. "These

are painful decisions," concedes UC spokesman Mike Alva, "but you have to make decisions to retain quality and access in these tough times."

"The students feel we've done this to them," says longtime UC Regent Roy Brophy. "I share their frustration, but ... economic downfall is a faceless crime."

Officials also maintain that, even with the fee increases, students in California still get a better deal than their counterparts in other states. According to the state Department of Finance, fees at both CSU and UC remain lower than those for resident students at competing institutions in other states. Wilson himself says the two systems remain "a good deal" despite the escalation in fees. The administration makes an even stronger case for the community colleges, which have historically had the nation's lowest fees. If Wilson's proposed $7 per unit fee hike is approved by the Legislature, community college fees will still, according to the administration, be the third lowest in the nation.

"Community colleges, even at the level of fees proposed in our budget, are an extraordinary bargain," says Ray Reinhard, Wilson's assistant secretary for child development and education.

Comparisons with other states, however, are little comfort to the students and parents who are writing larger checks or borrowing more. According to the California Student Aid Commission, California college students took out a record $1.24 billion in new loans in the last six months of 1993 — a 50 percent jump over the same period in 1993. Other students find them-

selves working longer and longer hours, and some risk being priced out of college altogether.

As the check gets larger, meanwhile, course and section offerings diminish. Thousands of course sections have been cut system-wide at CSU, forcing an increasing number of students to extend their education an extra year in order to meet their major's course requirements.

Since 1990 community colleges have reduced the number of course sections by 10 percent. More specialized courses — such as certain foreign languages, design and graphic arts — were eliminated to make way for more offerings in core courses, such as math, science, and English. Even then, college officials report long lines and scheduling difficulties.

It doesn't take an economics major to figure out what happens when fees go up and course offerings go down: students bail. Enrollment at CSU dropped 6 percent last year, with 22,000 fewer students attending classes — 13,000 of them full-time students. UC lost only 2 percent of its 125,000 students in 1993, a change not surprising given that UC students tend to come from more affluent homes than those attending CSU. Most shocking was the decline in enrollment at community colleges — down 137,000 students, or 9 percent of the more than 1.5 million attending these schools. About 40 percent of those were students who already had bachelor's degrees and were taking courses either for enrichment or for retraining. Many of these students checked out after the Legislature approved a $50 per unit "differential fee" for post-baccalaureate students.

A Decade of Growth in Undergraduate Student Fees

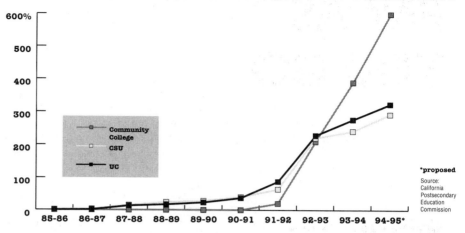

*proposed
Source: California Postsecondary Education Commission

What makes the enrollment drops at CSU and community colleges especially striking is that they occur at a time when the pressure for increased enrollment should be overwhelming. Not only is the state's population growing, but fee increases at the more expensive institutions have traditionally fueled enrollment at the less expensive schools. The economic downturn itself should have caused community college enrollments to soar, as those forced out of work by the recession go back to school for retraining. Yet, the trend continues downward.

"Part of the bargain of the Master Plan ... was to provide an open access to community college," notes Charles Cabaldon, chief consultant for the Assembly Higher Education Committee. "We're losing a whole bunch of students for whom community college were intended."

Recognizing the barriers to access that can be created by sharp fee increases during a recession, all three systems have accompanied their hikes with hefty increases in financial aid. Since 1990 roughly one-third of every additional fee dollar has gone into the financial aid pool at UC, CSU and the community colleges. UC Regent William Bagley says the fee increases have allowed the university "to provide full aid to cover the needy student." Financial-aid dollars have doubled at community colleges since 1990, and CSU officials claim a more than five-fold increase over the same period. "We've been forced to confront a reality that's been hidden," says Ray Reinhard. "A dollar saved to a family that can pay more is a dollar denied to a student who really needs it."

Critics say the financial aid backfill doesn't nearly make up for the impact of the fee hikes, particularly on middle-income students. While UC enrollment of low-income students has risen from 25 percent to 29 percent, the university has lost students with family incomes in the $50,000 to $70,000 range. Changes in the eligibility criteria, including a recent one more closely tying aid to parents' income, have hit students especially hard.

"This recession has been a white-collar, professional, middle-class recession," notes Callan. "It has struck right at the heart of people who have been to college, and who send their kids to college."

While they insist they are making adjustments to better account for the hard-luck cases, officials concede that students with family incomes above $50,000 will likely have to either work or borrow more. Still, they steadfastly maintain that the new fee structure is infinitely better than allowing the quality of instruction to erode any further than it may have already.

"We recognize that may be difficult," notes UC spokesman Alva, "but we believe that by maintaining the quality of the institution, the sacrifices will be worth it."

Student groups also believe the colleges and universities haven't done enough to cut administrative and non-essential costs. The issue is particularly touchy at UC, where critics have long charged that professors don't spend enough time in the classroom. "There are cost-containment efforts on campuses, but there's no system-wide commitment to cost containment," says Sara Swan with the UC Students Association. "They're only looking at fees."

"The usual view in higher education is that quality is a function of how much money you spend, and if you increase productivity, you give up quality," says Callan. "That has to be challenged."

Officials in all three systems vigorously deny that they've ignored cost containment. UC claims to have cut nearly half a billion dollars from its budgets over the last four years, and UC President Jack Pelatson says the institution is undergoing "a serious restructuring of the way we go about our business." CSU's downsizing in course offerings has been accompanied by a significant administrative downsizing. "Just last year," says CSU spokesman Steve MacCarthy, "our central administration took a 20 percent cut, and campuses took a 1.5 percent to 2 percent cut."

Still, the criticism resonates in the ears of the CSU Board of Trustees and the UC Regents, who make the policy decisions and must face the phone calls from frustrated students, parents and legislators. Before voting for the new UC fee policy, several regents made it clear they are watching the administration closely, and expect fee rollbacks to be the top priority if more state dollars become available. "I'm concerned that we're going to end up being the most expensive public education system in the country," says

Brophy. "This can't go on."

Much of this rhetorical thrust-and-parry, of course, is for the benefit of the Legislature and the governor, who have the ultimate power to shape student fee policy. Last year, CSU's four-year master fee plan suffered a setback when the Legislature chopped its 37 percent fee increase to 10 percent. This year's $340 proposed increase should face similar scrutiny, as lawmakers are suspicious about the concept of tying fees to a certain percentage of the cost of instruction. Fee policy is also expected to be at the center of a higher education "summit," which new Senate President pro Tempore Bill Lockyer (D-Hayward) says is planned for later in the spring. The summit is expected to be modeled after last year's economic "summit" organized by Assembly Speaker Willie Brown Jr.

Prospects for keeping the fees down, however, depend largely on the success of Governor Wilson's request for $3 billion in additional federal assistance. The prospects for such a bailout are considered "iffy" at best. Even if that money comes through and the state's economy turns around, however, virtually everyone associated with higher education concedes the days of the "low cost, high quality" system envisioned by the Master Plan seem doomed.

"When you look at the increasing number of students coming out of secondary schools, and the limited amount of state dollars ... the pressure on student fees is going to be tremendous," says Dr. Warren Fox, executive director of the California Postsecondary Education Commission.

What's left for policymakers, then, is the same awful conundrum — hike fees and further threaten access, or roll fees back and possibly threaten the value of the degree itself. With those in charge of higher education continuing to insist that there's no fat left to be cut, students and their advocates see nothing but more and larger fee increases in the years ahead. These increases, they believe, will further strain the already tenuous link between the vision of the Master Plan and the realities of the recession-ravaged 1990s.

"The original idea was that public higher education would be affordable by all Californians who were qualified," says state Senator Tom Hayden (D-Santa Monica). "We now have a means test."